Geography
in the School Grounds

Learning through Landscapes

RALPH HARE
—— **CHRISTINE ATTENBOROUGH** ——
TREVOR DAY

Learning through Landscapes (LTL) is a national charity which aims to encourage and enable improvement to the educational use and environmental quality of school grounds for the benefit of children, schools and society as a whole. LTL provides information and training, produces publications, carries out research and is a membership organization.

For further details, please contact:

The Information and Publicity Officer
Learning through Landscapes
Third Floor, Southside Offices
The Law Courts
Winchester, Hampshire
SO23 9DL

Tel: (01962) 846258

We are particularly grateful to Ordnance Survey for its sponsorship of this publication.
Learning through Landscapes receives support from the Department of the Environment under its Environmental Action Fund

SOUTHGATE

First published 1996 by Southgate Publishers Ltd
Reprinted 1998.

Southgate Publishers Ltd
15 Barnfield Avenue, Exmouth,
Devon EX8 2QE

Printed and bound in Great Britain
by Short Run Press Ltd, Exeter, Devon.

British Library Cataloguing in Publication Data
A CIP catalogue record for this book is available from
the British Library.

ISBN 1–85741–023–8

ACKNOWLEDGEMENTS
Photographs and other illustrations are reproduced by
permission of the following:
p.11 (top) Devon Curriculum Advice
p.11 (bottom) Liz Gadd, Knowle Primary School
p.12 Photo Air
p.16 Ailsa Addicott, Combe Martin School, Devon
p.17 'My World' print-out: Sandford Primary School,
Devon
p.27 Elisabeth McGill, Ladysmith School, Exeter
p.36 Plan of Molehill Copse School, Kent: Learning
through Landscapes
p.43 Heathcoat Primary School, Tiverton, Devon
p.48 Cross-section: Buckfastleigh Primary School,
Devon
p.53 (top) Mural at St Nicholas R.C. School, Exeter:
Express & Echo Publications Ltd
p.53 (bottom) Pilgrim Primary School, Plymouth
p.54 Site plan: Heathcoat Primary School, Tiverton,
Devon
pp.60 and 65 Lipson Vale Primary School, Plymouth
Other photographs are by Learning through
Landscapes
Cover photograph: LTL
Every effort has been made to contact copyright
owners of illustrations used and the authors and
publisher apologize to any whose rights have
inadvertently not been acknowledged.

Contents

Examples of the types of questions that support geographical enquiry

What is it?) Where is it?) What is it like?) Who is involved?) When did it happen?)	These questions gather **Information**
Why is it like this?) How did it happen?) How do we explain it?) Why are they doing this?)	These questions provide **Explanation**
How might things change?) What might be the effect?) What do I expect to find?) What decisions need to be made?) What could be the consequences?)	These questions allow **Prediction**
What do I think and feel about this?) What do people think and feel about this?) What can I do?)	These questions encourage **Evaluation**

Geographical enquiry

Stage of enquiry	Example at Key Stage 1	Example at Key Stage 2
Identify a question, problem or issue.	Sometimes the younger children in the school get bored at playtime.	The school needs a place in the grounds for music and drama performances.
Ask relevant questions and suggest some likely answers.	Which children get bored? How often? Why is there a problem? What is provided to stimulate play? Perhaps too little is provided to promote good play. Maybe children have not learned the playground games of their parents.	What size should the stage be? Where should it be located? Will it disturb neighbours? Will the site hold the whole school community? A place needs to be found that provides a natural focal point, with the potential for those seated to see it.
Collect data and information to answer the questions.	Survey playtimes for a week, recording play activities on a map, with photographs. Interview staff and mealtime assistants. Tape record pupils' views, use a questionnaire.	Survey the grounds for possible sites. Cost any structural alterations required. Gather the school community's views of the proposal through interviews and questionnaires.
Present the results.	Make a wall display of the current activities. Summarize the results of the questionnaire in the display.	Graph the questionnaire results. Provide maps of short-listed sites with sketches of resulting landscape changes. Show breakdown of costs for each location.
Describe, explain and interpret the results. See how close your 'likely answers' were.	Discuss in class what the display shows and why there is a problem. Compare with the class's earlier ideas.	Describe and explain what the graphs, maps and costings show. Compare with your original ideas.
Draw conclusions.	Suggest ways in which playtime could be improved.	Rank the possible sites in order and produce a proposal for the governors to discuss.
Evaluate the enquiry.	Institute the suggested changes and carry out a similar survey six months later to see if play has changed.	How well was the enquiry carried out? Did it produce a well-thought-out, persuasive proposal? Did it lead to action?

Introduction

Aims and activities

School grounds can provide a stimulus and setting for a wide range of activities for teaching Geography in primary schools. This book contains suggestions for such activities and, as necessary, also explains the geographical context. The links between the various activities and the Programmes of Study for England and Wales and the Scottish Curriculum are shown in the chart on pages 66–9. Although Geography is the centrepiece of the activities there are many links across the curriculum especially with English, Mathematics, Science, Art and Technology. In Scotland, the activities in this book will be appropriate for Environmental Studies 5–14 – Understanding People and Place.

The book is structured so that it relates clearly to the National Curriculum for England and Wales. The chart on pages 66–9 also enables it to be easily used in Scotland. Chapter 2 focuses on the key geographical skills associated with mapwork. The other chapters also make liberal use of mapwork skills, for mapwork is vital to help tackle geographical questions, problems and issues and not just an end in itself. Other important skills, such as geographical enquiry and fieldwork skills are incorporated in nearly all activities in some form or other. Chapters 3 and 4 are centred on physical and human geography themes, while Chapter 5 tackles environmental aspects of the subject. Finally, Chapter 6 concentrates on helping children to develop a sense of place.

Each chapter contains photocopiable pages, designed for use by the pupils in the school grounds, but many of them could also be used elsewhere.

Some activities are suitable for use at both Key Stages 1 and 2, others for one or the other, in which case the key stage is indicated in the text. Teachers will want to select and carefully match activities to the needs, interests and capabilities of their pupils and may want to adapt them to particular situations.

References have been made throughout to the use of information technology, as it is an important requirement of the National Curriculum in Geography. There are many opportunities to use information technology in support of learning in Geography while working in the school grounds.

For many of the activities in this book you will find it helpful to have:
(a) maps of the school grounds at various scales and levels of detail;
(b) a grid chalked or painted on the playground (see page 13);
(c) a model of your school grounds (see page 9).

It is particularly helpful to draw your own school base map, perhaps at A3 or A4 size, which can be photocopied, enlarged and reduced, and the appropriate scales and details marked on. You then have a variety of school grounds plans which can be photocopied for groups or individual children as required. The easiest way to do this is to work from an existing map.

Ordnance Survey provide a site-centred large scale mapping service called Superplan at a discount of 10 per cent for educational establishments. For a list of approved Educational Suppliers contact the Ordnance Survey Education Team (see page 70 for address). L.E.A. funded schools are able to access large-scale maps held in their parent authorities' archives, and are able to photocopy maps under the terms of the L.E.A.'s copyright licence. Schools not funded by an L.E.A. will need to purchase a copyright licence before making photocopies. Alternatively, if you have to start from scratch you could lay out a grid of tapes or string across the school grounds (depending on their size) and draw first boundaries and then features on a scale grid.

Using and developing your school grounds

The school grounds encompass the whole site, the buildings and all the land and features within the perimeter boundary. The influence and impact of each school, however, does not stop at the boundary fence. The school is inextricably linked with the surrounding area. Most activities in the book illustrate this holistic approach. A number of activities might also be used on fieldwork to more distant locations, such as field centres.

Many of the activities could be used in almost any school grounds. The implication of well-planned use of your grounds is, however, that, the more imaginatively they are developed, the greater will be the opportunities for teaching Geography and many other subjects.

Learning through Landscapes' research has shown that sustainable school grounds development occurs when your school community:

- takes a long term view about what is possible;
- involves children at every possible stage, helped by teachers, parents and other adults;
- involves parents and the wider community;
- sees the grounds as a valuable resource for the widest possible range of activities involving the widest possible group of people.

Using and developing the school grounds is a very real kind of Geography in action. Further ideas and advice on developing your school grounds can be found in Learning through Landscapes' publications. Of particular relevance to Geography are the activities in the *Esso Schoolwatch* pack which promotes among other things, a careful audit of the grounds.

The geographer's approach

From a geographer's perspective, the school site can be seen in a number of ways. Each school site is an individual place with its own distinctive character. Even schools built to a similar design gain their own personality over time, not least because of the individuality of their occupants.

When seen from above, that special geographical viewpoint, the school site presents a medley of patterns – lines, dots, patches – some of which are semi-permanent and deliberately designed, such as the shape of buildings, while others, such as the distribution of children in the playground, may seem as randomly distributed as confetti at a wedding.

The school site also has its own landscape. Geographers, of course, have a tradition of studying landscapes. Developing this concept of landscape, geographers study how people interact with their various environments. People affect the environment both for the better and for the worse. Similarly, people are affected by their environment. The school grounds, therefore, play their part in this interaction.

How geographers study is equally important. Geographical enquiry is both a central component of the National Curriculum and the Scottish 5–14 Curriculum and a guiding tool for geographers. At its simplest for children, it involves asking a range of pertinent questions, as shown in the chart at the top of page 4. Older children can be involved in a more structured approach which sets up and tests hypotheses and allows generalizations to be formed. This is illustrated in the lower chart on page 4. Geographical enquiry has been used throughout this book as a means of helping children investigate the school site.

Although there is a separate chapter focusing on mapwork skills, they are in nearly every case combined with the themes of Geography and based, of course, on the very real place that is your school. This combination of skills, places and themes is the very essence of National Curriculum Geography.

The need for schools to make better use of their school grounds for geography is emphasized in the OFSTED report *Geography: A Review of Inspection Findings 1993/94*. One of the key issues it suggests for schools is: 'More opportunities should be taken for investigative and field work in the school grounds …'

The school site is a rich and rewarding place for geographical learning. There are many worthwhile activities for undeveloped sites as well as those where the grounds have been specifically developed for learning in Geography and other subjects.

Mapwork Skills

Most maps are not easy for children to understand or use. It is important that children are introduced to mapwork at an early age through activities which help to develop basic concepts such as location, direction, scale and representation.

Mapwork involves children in:
- having some understanding of scale;
- using symbols that are not necessarily familiar;
- recognizing features and where they are in relation to each other;
- understanding direction and having knowledge of the points of the compass;
- seeing the world from another perspective;
- developing a visual memory;
- learning to enjoy maps;
- visualizing an image of a place represented on a map;
- developing their understanding of space.

Children also have to be helped to see the many ways in which maps are useful. The school grounds offer plenty of opportunities for this.

Maps may be used or made for:
- recording data, e.g. showing where different trees are located (KS1);
- measurements of temperature (KS2);
- showing patterns of distribution, e.g. where the litter bins are (KS1), where children gather to play quietly, sit or run around at breaktime (KS2);
- communicating information to others in a visual form, e.g. to link with photographs, illustrating 'Our favourite places in school' (KS1), or as part of a school prospectus designed by the children (KS2);
- guiding other people, e.g. following a specific route around the school in a treasure hunt (KS1), designing a board which shows visitors the layout of the school (KS2).

These and many other map-making ideas are included throughout the book, illustrating where maps can be purposefully made or used for particular reasons. This chapter aims to show how the school grounds may be used to help develop skills related to the making, understanding and use of maps.

Beginning mapwork

The school grounds can provide an effective starting point for young children learning about maps. Children will gain valuable experiences from taking part in structured play activities including the use of models, such as farms, road and building layouts, construction toy models and homemade models of real or fictional places, playmats and movable toys. These experiences will prepare children for activities which are based on the larger scale of the school grounds, and beyond.

SIGNPOST MAPPING
This activity aims to help both Key Stage 1 and early Key Stage 2 children improve their understanding of where they are in relation to other features around them.

Ask children to think about what a signpost does – it shows the direction of an object or a place from where you are standing. Get children to use their arms as directional signposts both in the classroom and outside. (For young children a more limited and defined area is easier to start off in.) Ask them to indicate where objects, such as a tree, door, bench or pond, are from where they are standing, without turning around or moving.

Compare two children who are in different parts of the playground. Did they both use the same arm? If not, why not? Which child is nearer to/further away from the particular object? The direction and the distance of something from you depends very much on where you are in the first place: the bench

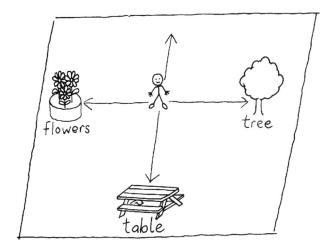

Young children can use simple drawings to practise signpost mapping.

hasn't moved but the two children are in different places in the playground. Children can then practise pointing to two objects at the same time.

Encourage children to identify the direction in which an object is: for example, 'The bench is in front of me but the swings are behind me'. Small games can be played using this vocabulary: for example, 'Everyone stand so that the road is behind you and the front door is in front of you' or 'the gate is to your left and the tree is to your right'.

Once children are confident in these activities they can begin to record what they have done on paper, using a cross or a stick person to represent themselves in the centre of the paper, with an arrow showing the way they are facing (you may wish to draw this for them). They will have to turn the paper so that the arrow is pointing away from them. Ask the children to mark on three features which they have first pointed to and use arrows on the paper to show which way they pointed their arms. Using this method, children can start to put together maps of a small area such as part of the playground as it looks from where they are sitting.

You could also ask the children to think of places or objects they cannot see, but know well, and consider their position in relation to where the children are: for example, 'Which direction is the playground or the hall from the classroom?' or 'Where is the car park from the playground?'

This activity is developed further for Key Stage 2 children in 'Creating a toposcope' on page 18.

A VIEW FROM ABOVE

During Key Stage 1, teachers will want to introduce children to the idea of looking at objects from above in order to help them understand the way in which sketch maps and plans work.

Placing objects on an overhead projector, shielded from the gaze of the children, presents a good opportunity for guessing games which involve identifying everyday objects seen from an unusual viewpoint. This will help to establish the concept of a plan view.

You could arrange place settings of knives, forks and spoons to be shown on the overhead projector and challenge children to recognize and rearrange them.

Other 'mystery' objects, such as pieces of doll's house furniture and flat or 3D shapes, or everyday items such as a pencil, comb or coin, can be placed on the projector for them to guess at. Children need to see the objects from a variety of angles. Ask them to guess at which way up the item is and also to suggest how the shadow may change as the shape is moved around.

You could ask the children to collect objects from outside to use in the game. This will encourage them to notice the shapes of things outside as they look for suitable items.

Extend the activity by matching outline shapes of objects to the objects themselves.

A shapes plan of the playground

Challenge the children to draw the shadow they think they will see before an object is put on the projector.

You can then move on to larger objects in the classroom and outside. Ask the children to decide which, of a variety of plastic or card shapes, would best represent items such as tables, chairs and wastepaper bins found in the classroom, and benches, trees, pond, litter bins and so on found outside. Can they make a simple shapes map of the playground on a large sheet of paper?

Encourage the children to observe the shadows cast by objects in the playground, such as goal posts, branches, railings. Can they predict what shadow an object will cast?

HUNT THE SHAPE

Take children on a walk around the school, looking for objects whose view from above (plan view) would match particular shapes. For example, a rectangular plan view might fit such objects as a picnic table, a bench or a car, a circular plan view might include a drain cover or the pond, while a square might represent paving stones, the bird table or the playground. These could be recorded pictorially or on a chart.

Using models

One of the most difficult aspects of mapwork is that of scale and yet it is something children are very familiar with through a wide variety of toys. Both scale and plan view (or 'bird's eye view') can be successfully approached through the use of models. The following activities are based on using a model of the school site, but the activities suggested are transferable to other scale models, such as a classroom model, a playmat layout, or a model of a place visited or of a fictional place. Such activities may usefully be undertaken with both younger and older children.

Create opportunities for young children to look down at objects wherever possible – for example, from an upstairs window, or by standing on a table or chair or piece of P.E. apparatus – and let them trace in the air or draw the main shape they see each time.

Rather than ask children to try to draw an area of the school grounds as a bird might see it, start by building a simple, large model on or in a cardboard box. It needs to be

made so that the sides can be let down to see the area from the side.

CLASSROOM MODEL

In preparation for the playground modelling activity explained below, try creating a simple model of the classroom first of all. This is particularly appropriate for Key Stage 1 but may be equally suitable for older children who still need to develop the plan view concept. This could include:

- making small items of furniture and fittings to go in the room;
- turning the model round (orientating it) until it matches the actual room;
- viewing the model from above and drawing the layout from this position. It is easier if, in the first instance, a frame is drawn on paper for the children. This should be the same size as the outside measurement of the model, indicating the edges of the room and perhaps one reference point, such as a particular piece of furniture.

PLAYGROUND MODEL

What does your playground look like? Whatever its size and shape it is likely to have some boundary walls, hedges or railings and is therefore probably a fairly enclosed area which will lend itself to modelling in the way outlined above. You can start from a box shape or alternatively use a

A model playground made from a cardboard box

cut-out cardboard outline to represent the shape of your school grounds.

Get the children to find out what is actually in the playground and where it is placed, by marking litter bins, play equipment and seats, for example, on an outline plan or on the model base itself. Information could also be taken from aerial photographs of the school, but children should still refer to the real place in order to interpret this.

Make small models to represent the features found and place them in the correct part of the model playground. The children could also make model people, representing themselves, and place them in the grounds. Ask them to describe where they are located and then where they would move them to. Ask them questions such as 'Where would you be if it was first thing in the morning/ you were eating lunch outside/playing football/reading/skipping?' and so on. Use the model figures to help the children explain how the playground is used.

Get the children to stand and look down at the model and to describe what they would see if they were a bird flying overhead. How would this change at different times of the day? What are the main shapes that are obvious from above? Ask the children to try drawing their own 'view from above' of the playground, within a prepared outline, concentrating on the outline shapes made by the main features. Their plans could be drawn on the computer.

Introduce some problem solving. Ask the children what they like doing best outside and then where they do it. What do they dislike doing? Are there aspects of the grounds which they would like to remove or change, or things they would like to add?

Give the children, in groups, a new item for the model playground, such as a climbing frame, a new table and bench or a playhouse, and ask them to decide where would be the best place for it. When they have decided, they must justify their decision to the other groups. Why have they chosen a particular place?

Alternatively, give groups of children an outline shape of the present playground and the task of redesigning it based on the class discussion about their grounds. This will work much better if they model their ideas first and then draw a plan from the model afterwards. Models are easier to compare

and discuss and features can be moved around more easily than on a plan.

BLUE MONKEY
This activity can be carried out with a model or an outline of the playground. Place a grid (approximately 6 x 6, and not bigger than 10 x 10) on top of the model playground.

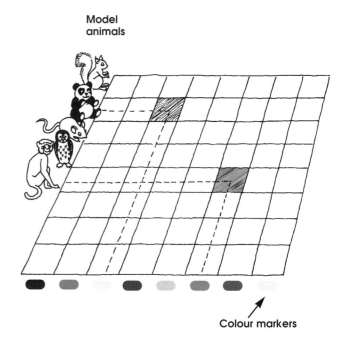

Model animals

Colour markers

This grid could be chalked on the tarmac itself or drawn on a base model of the playground.

The grid could be drawn on a piece of clear acetate. Put a different model animal (or shape) at the end of each row and a different colour marker in each column. Get the children to identify the square of the green lion, the blue monkey, the red squirrel or whatever.

A natural extension of this is to introduce letter/number co-ordinates and eventually number/number co-ordinates. (To take this game outside, refer to the playground games section on page 13.)

A MODEL SCHOOL
A model of the school and its grounds is full of potential for teaching mapwork and many other aspects of geography as well as other areas of the curriculum. Much exciting and successful work, at both key stages, can be achieved using simple models built by the children as well as more durable and accurate wooden scale models which could be

A model of a school site using various wooden shapes

constructed by a practical parent or commissioned from a professional model maker. One enterprising reception teacher built a simple but strong wooden model based on a box structure which was big enough for young children to walk around.

COMPARING THE MODEL WITH THE SITE
Let the children consider things which are around the school but are not represented on the model – litter bins, flower beds, playground markings, the pond, for example. Using a simple plan of the school site, they can go outside and mark the position of these features on the plan and then relate it to the model in order to make and add new details to it.

If the model is built to scale, older Key Stage 2 children can use it for measuring and scale-related activities, such as estimating and then working out distances from one point in the grounds to another, or measur-

ing the perimeter of the playground, field or school site. These measurements can then be compared with those they take around the school site. How accurate is the model?

Models and photographs

HELICOPTER FLIGHT
Before using the model for this activity take a series of photographs of it from different heights and angles.

For Key Stage 1 children, give each of them a photograph and ask them to 'fly in a helicopter' to find out where the photograph was taken from. They could even use a toy helicopter to fly over the model. Children may need to get to the same height as the adult who took the photos, so supervised use of a chair or step ladder may be necessary.

Children could use an ION camera (this takes still video pictures) or a Polaroid camera to take their own aerial photos. Put the photos in order and compare them to see how the features of the model change with height. Ask the children if they can identify features that can be seen at ground level but not from above. What can be seen from above which is not visible from lower down? Use a real aerial photograph of the school and compare that with an aerial view of the model. What can be seen in the school photograph which does not appear on the model? Can the model be added to and improved by comparing these photographs?

Take the model outside to help in identifying the exact shape, size and position of missing features.

Develop this activity further at Key Stage 2 by considering the plan view shapes which would be used to represent the different parts of the school. If each part of the model is movable and can be drawn around, the plan shape becomes much more obvious.

Provide sketches of parts of the model as seen from above as well as from the more familiar side views and oblique views. Ask the

Children can choose model play equipment for the site model.

Oblique aerial photo of a school in central London

children to match each sketch to the model. Extend this by getting the children to match a plan of the school to the model. They will need to orientate the plan to the model. You could then provide an incomplete plan and get the children to sketch in the missing parts, or play 'Spot the difference' using a plan which has some inconsistencies.

Vertical photo of a school and its undeveloped grounds

PHOTO SPOT

Make a collection of photographs of places around the school site. These should include some shots of small features at unusual angles as well as more recognizable places.

Ask the children to identify where in the school they think these places are, then take them out to check. At each photo spot decide where the photographer was when the photo was taken. Older children can use a compass to establish which direction the photographer faced to take each photo and also to decide the direction from the school of particular views.

As each place is identified, Key Stage 2 children could be asked to mark the photo spot on a school plan and then relate the information on this to the school model once back in the classroom. Alternatively, with younger children, the model could be taken outside and the photo spots identified and marked immediately. It is important to orientate the model to match the part of the school you are in.

These photos, or ones taken by pupils, can be scanned into the computer (or you could use still video pictures, saved as 'Sprites') and transferred to a program such as 'Magpie'. Older Key Stage 2 children can use this to compile an information file on places around the school, using text, pictures and possibly sound, for younger children to access.

Relate features within the site to a school plan by a display of photos linked to a large plan. If you have the use of a concept keyboard and a program such as 'Touch Explorer Plus', it is relatively easy to set up an overlay featuring a plan of the school site for Key Stage 1 children to investigate. They could find out the names and/or details of particular features in the school grounds or they could use their knowledge of the plan to follow clues to find hidden objects.

PICTURE MAPPING

At Key Stage 1, take the children for a walk around your school site. Stop at a number of locations and look at, name and describe the particular features seen there. Get the children to take mental photographs of the feature or view, using their hands as a frame and opening and closing their eyes to 'take' the picture and store it in their memory.

Talk about where each feature is in relation to other features you have seen – distance away and compass direction. At a halfway point on your walk ask the children to try to recall the pictures they have taken so far and the order they came in.

On returning to the classroom go through the walk with the children. If you have photos of the features/views you looked at, try to sequence them as well. The children should then complete the worksheet (photocopiable page 20), by naming each location they stopped at and drawing their mental photograph from there.

At Key Stage 2, take the children for a walk or allow them to choose their own route through the grounds. Ask them to

Playground markings are useful and decorative.

make a record of six to eight features they think are interesting. They could do this by making simple sketches, talking into a tape recorder or using a still video camera or Polaroid camera. They then complete the worksheet, using their information.

Playground markings

These are useful for developing geographical skills as well as being fun to play on, and can be painted on a playground or other suitable area around the school. Children can be involved in planning and producing these, while at the same time practising important geographical skills.

GRIDS

A 10 x 10 or 12 x 12 grid is a very useful marking for a tarmac area. It can be marked out temporarily with playground chalk but it is much better if it is painted. Similar games to 'Blue monkey' (see page 10) can be played on a larger scale, providing a variety of ways to practise learning co-ordinates. Numbers and/or letters can be chalked on either spaces or lines to provide suitable co-ordinates for any age group. Cones, coloured discs, beanbags and so on can be used as markers or children themselves can stand on specified squares or points.

COLOUR BINGO

Mark the grid with suitable co-ordinates – shape/colour (as in 'Blue monkey'), letter/number or number/number – according to the understanding of the children.

Assemble the children in teams, each with a set of beanbags in a particular colour. The aim of the game is to place the beanbags in a straight line, either horizontally, vertically or diagonally. To achieve this the teams take turns to call out the grid reference of the square in which they wish to place their beanbag. One member of the team has to go and put the marker down. If it is put in the wrong place the team forfeits their turn. The first team to get three or four or, more difficult, five in a row, wins.

PLAYING WITH PATTERNS

Ask the children to produce simple patterns or pictures in colour on a 10 x 10 or 12 x 12 grid on squared paper. Identify coloured

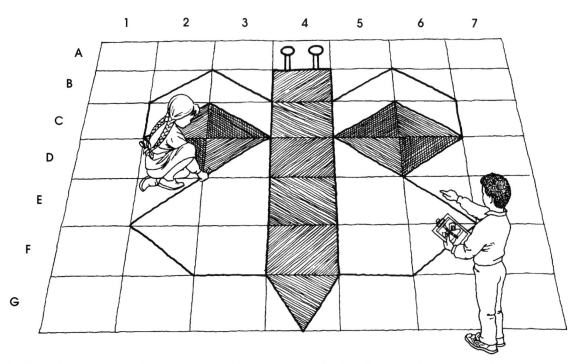

A simple picture or pattern designed on a grid on paper can be transferred on to a larger grid on the playground.

squares by their co-ordinates: for example, A1 is blue, C6 is green. Now let the children instruct each other in reconstructing their patterns on the playground grid or on a number of smaller chalked grids, by calling out a pair of co-ordinates and the appropriate colour. The square could be coloured in, using chalk, in order to provide some instant, but temporary, playground art.

MAPPING A MINIATURE SCHOOL
An enlarged plan of the school site can be drawn on the playground by older Key Stage 2 children. First add a grid and co-ordinates to a plan of the school site drawn on paper. Then draw or paint the same grid, enlarged to the required size, on a tarmac area, adding co-ordinates to match those on the paper plan. Allocate one square of the plan to each child and let them reproduce the mapping in the square on the large grid using chalk. Once the enlarged plan is finished it can be painted over if you wish to keep it.

Alternatively, you could draw a school plan on a large offcut of plastic floor covering. This can be rolled up and put away easily and can be taken out and placed wherever it is required. It can be drawn on or used with a programmable toy such as a Roamer, PIP or PIXIE. Key Stage 1 children can be given structured play activities such as sending the toy from one point to another, turning it,

returning it to base and getting it to move around or between obstacles on the plan. At Key Stage 2 children can design sequences of movement and use compass points for directions and degrees for the turns made by the toy.

SIGNS AND DIRECTIONS
A project on direction and distance could be planned to develop your school grounds so that they are more accessible.

With the children, decide which places in and around the school site visitors and children want to get to reasonably frequently. Which are the most popular or most appropriate routes?

Using a variety of coloured shapes and footprints (both human and animal), paint signs on the ground to show the pathways between different places – for example, the front gate and the main entrance, the entrance and the playground. Signposts, placed at main entrances to the school, could also be designed so that the routeways are easily identifiable.

Ask the children to consider the distance of the routes you have identified in the grounds. Is one longer or shorter than another? Which route would involve the longest journey?

Key Stage 2 children can investigate actual distances between places in the grounds using metre tapes or a trundle wheel. As

A map of the school and its neighbourhood can be painted on the playground.

MAZES

Start by introducing children to a variety of ready-produced mazes, such as puzzle books of mazes which are based on different shapes. Then get the children to design their own. These may be painted on the ground or they could be built from brick, stone or banked soil, or low bushes could be grown to make a living maze (see the photos opposite page 36). They can be linked to work in Mathematics and English.

well as measuring the whole distance between two points they will also need to consider stages of the route, such as the distance to a turning point or where paths cross.

Mark the information, routeways and distances on a plan and use a model, if you have one, to decide where it would be most appropriate to put distance markers. These could be painted on boards or large pieces of rock.

COMPASS POINTS

Try designing an unusual eight-point compass which helps children to learn the directional terms. For example, an elephant incorporated into the design may help reinforce the mnemonic phrase 'Naughty Elephants Squirt Water'. It is important to check that the compass marking is pointing in the right direction before painting. Older children can check this using real compasses.

Other directional markings could be investigated and added to the compass or used as a separate design. For example, the direction of Mecca could be shown or you could make a complete compass of religious places.

Coloured footprints make effective direction markers.

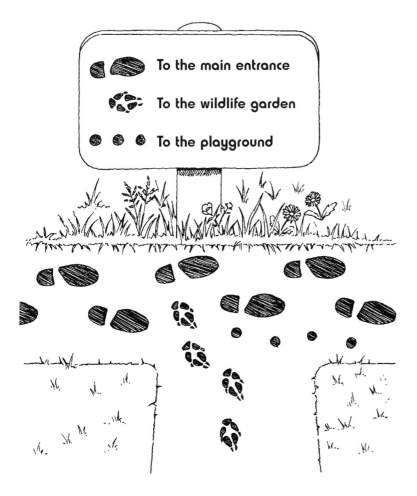

To the main entrance

To the wildlife garden

To the playground

COMPASS CHALLENGE

Ask each child to choose two different places in the school grounds and mark them on a school plan. Then go outside and at each place they have chosen ask them to use their compass to find North, then stand facing in that direction. They should mark on their worksheet (photocopiable page 21) the feature which is furthest away from them looking directly North. Then ask them to choose something in the middle distance and something close by and mark them on the worksheet also. Get them to estimate how far away each

An 'elephant' compass painted on the ground

FINDING YOUR WAY AROUND

School grounds provide suitable limited and safe areas to introduce orienteering. In Key Stage 1 you can work with layouts of equipment such as cones, ropes and other small apparatus. Children can use these layouts to learn to draw, orientate and use simple plans and to follow simple directions.

TREASURE HUNT

Give a small group of Key Stage 1 children a simple directional clue card which takes them from the classroom to the first of a number of points. (Non readers may need an older child or a helper with them.) The points should be specific, recognizable places at which an adult or older child may be positioned to help. The children should be aware that they have to follow a particular route and that at each place they will collect a new directional instruction. They might

feature is and write it down. Repeat this looking South, East and West. Back in the classroom try to identify the features on either a school site map, a local large scale map or a smaller scale map (e.g. Ordnance Survey. 1:25 000), depending on how far they could see. Can they work out more accurately the distance of each feature from their viewing point? Other ideas for playground markings can be found on pages 63–4.

Exploring the school grounds through maps

Children should have lots of opportunities through both key stages to use and become more familiar with the school plan. They can mark on information, such as the position of trees or litter bins, or use it to help them follow routes or to make decisions about changes to the site. In your geography resources include a variety of photocopiable school site plans, at different scales and with varying amounts of detail, such as the Ordnance Survey Superplans in the centre pages.

A treasure hunt clue card for Key Stage 1

Clue 1

**Out of the door
turn left ⬅
through the hall
turn right ➡**

also collect a letter or a jigsaw piece which will make a word or a picture if they find all the places correctly.

Alternatively, a group of children can be given a photo of a particular place in the school. They have to decide where it is and how to get there, mark their route and the point on a plan and proceed to the point to collect a second photo clue.

Ask older children to mark on a simple plan the places they arrive at. For example, they could colour in a room or mark a point with a letter or number. Can they draw in the route they took from one point to another?

Of course, at the end of all these trails should be some form of treasure!

AN ORIENTEERING COURSE

For Key Stage 2, set up a course around the school grounds for children to develop their compass skills. Each point can be marked by a coloured peg, a piece of material, a number tag or similar clear marker, with a crayon or stamp for recording. Working in pairs,

children are given a compass and a set of instructions for each part of the route, indicating the direction and the number of paces to walk. At each point the children record on their sheet (by colour, number, word or shape) and then follow the next set of directional instructions.

For example:

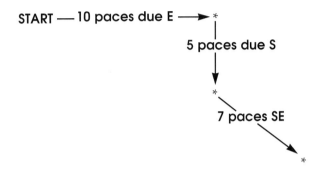

Once the children have had some experience of this they can design their own courses, in groups, for the rest of the class to try out.

At Sandford Primary School, 'My World' program has been used to create a plan of the whole school site.

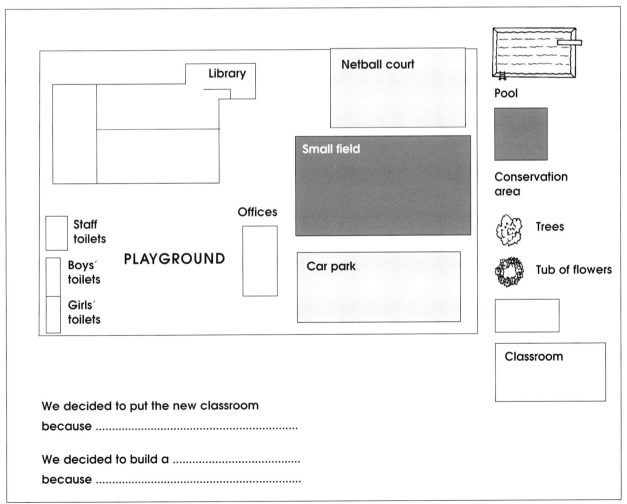

MY WORLD – MY SCHOOL

Produce a plan of the school using a vecto-graphics (modelling/drawing) computer program and turn it into an activity screen. This can be done by setting up some key features on a section of the plan on screen (for example, footprints or arrows for making routeways, outline shapes of litter bins, flower beds, classrooms, etc. for decision and planning tasks) and providing simple copying and placing instructions. If you use Acorn computers this can be done by using 'Draw'. Once a simple plan and set of features has been created in 'Draw' it can be combined with 'My World' program, to make activity screens for children to complete (see 'Routeways' below). The activities which are produced using 'My World' can be simple enough for Key Stage 1 children to use or made more complex for older children.

ROUTEWAYS

Set up the 'My World' program on the computer with a plan of the school and a set of footprint shapes which can be dragged on to the screen. Children take part in an activity such as a treasure hunt or an investigation into ways of getting to different parts of the school. They then use a print-out of the plan to mark out their ideas and then record them on the computer using the footprints to show the routeway they have chosen. The printed-out routeways plan can then be tested out, perhaps by other children. Alternatively, get one child to design a routeway on the screen, print it out and give it to another to follow. All screens can be saved and printed out, providing a useful means of assessing children's work.

CREATING A TOPOSCOPE

Every school has a view, no matter how restricted or localized, and a school built on top of a hill provides an ideal site for making a toposcope. A toposcope identifies places and features which can be seen (or not seen in some cases) in different directions from a viewpoint, together with their straight-line distance (as the crow flies).

Choose a suitable point (or points) in your grounds from which children can look out at the surrounding area. This may be outside or it could be from an upstairs window, although it may not be possible to get a 360° view from such a point.

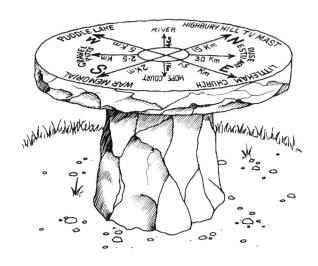

A toposcope

Signpost mapping can be used to good effect here with a variety of age groups. Younger children will need practice in using this first in simple activities such as those outlined on pages 7–8. For older children, you may find it helpful to use the 'Compass Challenge' worksheet (page 21) before starting this activity.

Encourage young children to use their arms to point out and name the physical and manmade features they can see. Help them to describe the position of these features using vocabulary such as 'far away', 'in the distance', 'near to us', 'between', 'behind me', 'in front of me' and so on. Alternatively, provide a set of photos of the views, taken in different directions, which the children can match to what they can see from the viewpoint.

Record the features that can be seen, very simply, using arrows to show direction and relative distance.

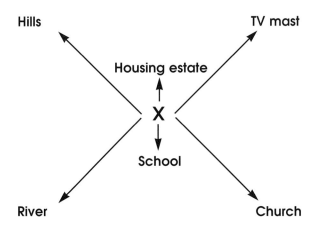

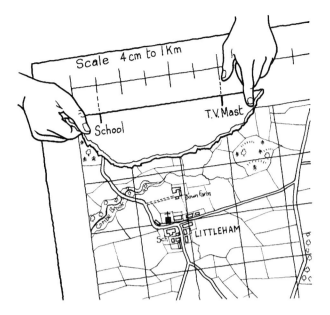

Finding the straight-line distance measurement

Give older children a compass and ask them to identify one feature that they can see to the N,S,E and W of where they are standing. Get them to record these features on their signpost map. How far away do they think each feature is? They can record their ideas on the relative distance arrows. How could they find out the true distance?

To help them answer this question, use a map extract of the view. For a limited view a large scale map, such as 1:10 000, would be suitable; for a wider and more distant view Ordnance Survey Pathfinder maps, at 1:25 000 scale, are very useful. Ask the children to look at the map and find the school site and then the features they have identified. Use the key to see how the features are represented.

Get the children to line up the school site viewpoint and the feature identified on the map with a straight edge of paper and to mark the two positions on the paper. If they then lay the paper along the map scale they should get an immediate answer. If you have copied and enlarged or

reduced a map extract, remember to enlarge or reduce the scale line by the same amount at the same time! (Always check that your L.E.A. has a licence which allows you to do this.) Questions such as 'What is the most distant feature we can see from our site?' and 'How far away is it?' can then be answered.

Other children can be given smaller scale maps and asked to find out which direction and how far away some more distant landmarks are from school.

This work will provide all you need to make a toposcope. Children can design a painted board for the viewpoint as a new feature for your grounds, or it could be painted directly on the ground if there is a suitable surface. Alternatively, the toposcope could be recorded on laminated cards and then used by younger children when looking out from the viewpoint.

By making a detailed plan of the school site children will learn useful mapping skills.

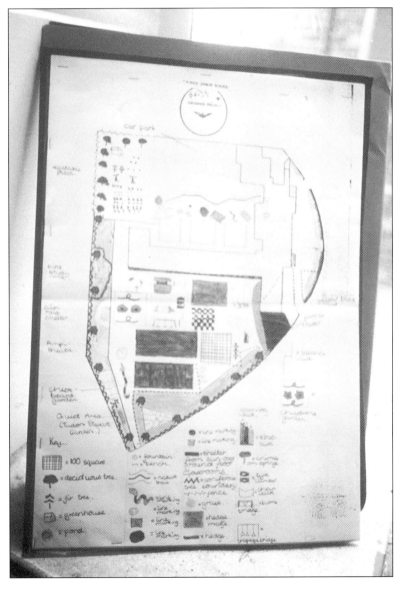

A Walk Around Our School Grounds

At _____
the view looked like this.

At _____
the view looked like this.

At _____
the view looked like this.

At _____
the view looked like this.

At _____
the view looked like this.

At _____
the view looked like this.

Compass Challenge

Furthest away _____   Estimated distance _____

Actual distance _____

Middle   _____   Estimated distance _____

Actual distance _____

Close by   _____   Estimated distance _____

Actual distance _____

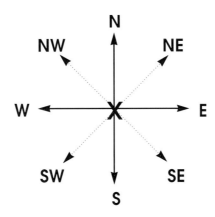

Weather, Water and Landforms

Weather and climate

'Another wet playtime!' This familiar phrase well illustrates the effect that the weather has on us and this is one of the reasons why we should study the weather. Measuring and recording the weather in the school grounds is a fruitful activity for children for all kinds of reasons, including the following:

- It provides opportunity for direct, first-hand observations.
- It generates original, unique data.
- It is cross-curricular.
- It encourages accurate and careful observation and recording.
- It helps children become familiar with scientific recording equipment and the application of I.T.
- It can be linked to multimedia enquiries, involving newspapers, television, radio, teletext and so on.
- It can be carried out with relatively simple, low-cost equipment.

A good starting point is to ask the children to think about the different elements that make up the 'weather'. These include temperature, sunshine, rainfall, wind and visibility. It is the day-to-day variation of these elements that makes our weather. The climate is the averages of these elements over a longer period, such as a month or a season.

The chart 'Weather watching', on the next page, could be used to introduce children to the different elements of the weather. Another starting point, at Key Stage 1, is to ask children where the windy places are, the sunny places, the cold ones, and so on. You can extend this by getting the children to think about the people who help to maintain the building, whatever the weather. The care-taker could be invited to talk to the children about how he/she thinks the weather affects the school.

- Which areas get most dirty when it is wet?
- What parts suffer from leaking roofs, draughty windows, etc.?
- Who is brought in to do the repairs?
- Where do all the leaves accumulate?

HOW DOES THE WEATHER AFFECT PEOPLE'S BEHAVIOUR?

The box on page 24 shows many of the ways that the weather affects us at school. Pupils could be asked to think about how the school and its grounds are designed to cope with the extremes of the weather. This could begin with a brainstorm:

- Are there any open corridors or passage-ways?
- Are doors and windows designed not to slam?
- Are there particularly windy areas outside where trees or fences could be planted for shelter?
- Does the design and siting of litter bins help to control litter or does it all get blown out?

Children at Key Stage 2 could then frame some central questions, such as 'How well does the school protect us from the weather?', which lead to a more structured investigation.

Observational work could include daily weather recordings and other observations made around the site, such as:

- (at Key Stage 2) building features, including door stays, weather strips and draught excluders around doors, sun blinds, double glazing, solar panels and electric fans;
- using sound meters to record noise levels from pupils during wet and dry playtimes;
- interviewing teachers to find out whether or not they think that pupils' behaviour changes according to the weather.

The results of this research could be put on a data base and displayed, and this could lead to discussion about how to carry out any improvements.

The photocopiable sheet on page 30 suggests another starting point that could be used with Key Stage 1 pupils.

WEATHER WATCHING		
Elements	Questions to ask	Impact on people
Temperature	How hot is it? How cold is it? How does it vary during the day?	How does it affect the things we do? What about heating bills? What clothes keep us warm?
Sunshine	How long does the sun shine each day?	How do we feel when it is: – bright and sunny? – grey and cloudy?
Rainfall	How much rain has fallen today/this week/this month? How long has it rained today?	What clothes keep us dry? How does a wet day make us feel? How do droughts affect us?
Wind	How strong is the wind today? What direction is the wind blowing from? Which winds seem to bring wet/dry/warm/cool weather?	How do we behave when there are strong winds? Which clothes protect us from the wind?
Visibility	How far can we see? Is the visibility good or poor when the wind is blowing/the air is still?	How do we feel when the view is cut out?

RECORDING THE WEATHER

Weather watching can also encourage children to measure and record accurately. A number of weather recording instruments can be made by the children themselves: see the anemometer on page 25, and the shadow clock (page 9) and the weather station (page 13) in *Science in the School Grounds*. Other items can be purchased for a reasonable price and will give accurate readings if used properly. Some educational suppliers produce automatic weather recording stations.

Pupils can display their weather recordings in a variety of ways. They could make their own weather board or use a commercially produced board. Some software, such as 'Weatherman', creates weather map screens that are appropriate for either key stage. 'Weather Station' is used more at Key Stage 2 since it generates a variety of formats and block and line graphs using the data that children input. 'Weatherwatch' allows pupils to manipulate data and comes complete with recording sheets and work cards.

Collecting data on the school site will also generate ideas for comparing weather records. Among the possibilities are:

- matching the weather forecasts from radio and television with what actually happens;
- comparing the school's data with that of a local weather station; pairing with another school, or network of schools, to share data as part of a twinning exercise;
- using I.T. to receive METFAX updates or to download information received from a weather satellite, perhaps by linking with a local secondary school. (The Meteorological Society provides METFAX on a subscription basis to schools.)

MICROCLIMATES

Different parts of the school site will experience different weather conditions throughout the

Reading the temperature in the school grounds

THE EFFECTS OF THE WEATHER

Which has the greater impact on school life?

| SUN OR RAIN? | HOT OR COLD? | CALM OR WINDY? |

When it's sunny ...

Children enjoy playtime and games.
Children and teachers feel bright and lively.
Classrooms may need sunblinds.
We need to be careful about sunburn.
It's more fun to be outside.
More parts of the site can be used.

When it's rainy ...

There are wet coats everywhere.
Children don't want to go outside.
Playtimes are noisier inside.
It is more difficult for teachers to prepare rooms for lessons.
Teachers are less likely to have a break.
Children may get wet coming to school.
Recording the rainfall is a dampening experience!
Some parts of the school get crowded, e.g. cloakrooms, corridors, doorways.

When it's hot ...

We all feel lazy.
It's difficult to concentrate.
We look forward to playtimes and lunchtime.
Some rooms are hot and stuffy.

When it's cold ...

Some rooms are poorly heated.
Children may have cold hands and feet.
We have to remember to shut doors.
Heating bills are higher.
Children are distracted by snow falling.
Snow collects in some parts of the playground.

When it's windy ...

Doors and windows may slam.
Children don't behave so well.
Leaves and litter collect in corners of the playground.
Rain makes a noise on the windows.

When it's calm ...

It's easier to open windows and doors.
We can hear other sounds more easily.
We are usually less irritated.

year. The combination of these varied elements forms a microclimate and will often explain why some parts of the school are liked better and used more by the children than other parts.

Weather extremes in the school grounds

This activity will help the children find places in the school grounds where extremes of weather are experienced. Where are the warmest and coolest places? Which places have the strongest and lightest winds?

The children will need thermometers and an accurate instrument to measure wind speed such as a portable anemometer or wind meter. Examples of these are shown in the photograph opposite, while the diagrams illustrate examples of homemade equipment.

Use a map or a model of the school to discuss the children's experiences. Can they pick out a variety of places which show the influences of temperature and wind? Do they have any ideas why? They might suggest that sheltered areas exposed to the sun could be warmest. Alternatively, they may know of a vent from a heater in a temporary classroom which provides a local hotspot. Shortlist five or six locations and choose two or three that are most likely to provide useful data.

Measure and record temperature and wind strength at intervals during the day at each location. The children should also record anything they think might influence temperature and wind, such as sunshine or sheltering walls.

Data could be displayed as graphs located on the map of the school or entered on a simple spreadsheet and displayed on different print-outs.

Analyse the results. How wide are the variations from place to place? Do they change during the day? How can this be explained? What is the significance of the results? Do the temperature and wind variations affect where children prefer to sit? Do they affect play, plant growth or the choice of location for the school pond?

Other weather variables could be measured, such as the wettest and driest places and the sunniest and shadiest places. All these extremes could be marked on a microclimate wall map of the school.

A weather-friendly school?

Children can compare the results of the above activity with the school building design. Have features been built in the right place? Look, for example, at porches, sun roofs, paths, doors (designed to cope with wind gusts) and windows (to maximize sunlight). Are there different design needs in different seasons? How can we improve the

Anemometer and rain gauge on a school site

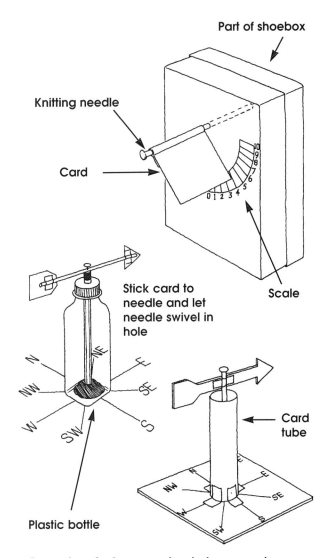

Examples of a homemade wind vane and an anemometer

site to take advantage of the good features of the microclimate and to minimize the bad features? What can be done at no, or low, cost?

An investigation into the influences of the microclimate could be extended by surveying different surfaces, for example:

- brick/stone
- tarmac
- short grass/play areas
- long grass/nature areas
- concrete

Ask the children to time how long it takes an ice cube to melt on each type of surface. They could plot the surfaces and times on a site plan. Which surfaces help the ice to melt most quickly?

SEASONS

Seasonal changes take longer to observe and their recording relies on accurate observation

In the summer the school grounds may be used for a concert.

could be completed by fixing cards on a circular calendar. It might form the starting point for artwork and written work for wall display.

Water on the school site

By studying what happens to the rainwater as it falls on the site children can be introduced to many different concepts:

- Water always flows downhill.
- Water flows will join together and form channels.
- Water soaks into the ground, but at different rates over different surfaces and soil types.
- Some surfaces and soils are impermeable so that the water stays on the surface, forming puddles or ponds.

Falling rain (and snow) is one part of the water cycle that is easy to see. It can be used to introduce children to different features of the school buildings that have been designed to cope with rainfall.

WHERE DOES THE WATER GO?
On a map of the school site, Key Stage 2 children can:

- shade in all the areas where the water runs off the surface in one colour;
- shade in all the areas where the water soaks into the ground in another colour;
- mark on the gutters around the roofs, the downpipes and the drains;

as well as on memory. Many of the school's activities throughout the year are linked to the seasons and the typical climatic conditions.

A chart like the one below could be used to show the main events in the school year, the likely weather and how the events will affect the school site. Possible events include:

Religious festivals
Harvest festivals
Sports days/tournaments
Christmas parties
Summer fêtes/garden parties
Hallowe'en
Christmas shopping car parking
Summer camps (on school field)
Car boot sales

You could also include events such as parents' evenings which will not make any impact (apart from parking perhaps). The activity

SCHOOL WEATHER CALENDAR			
School year	**Activity**	**Expected weather**	**Effect on school grounds**
November 5th	Bonfire party	Cold (and possibly wet)	Safe bonfire site needed to avoid damage to grounds – away from trees, planted areas and buildings
December			
January			
February			

WHAT HAPPENS TO THE RAINDROPS

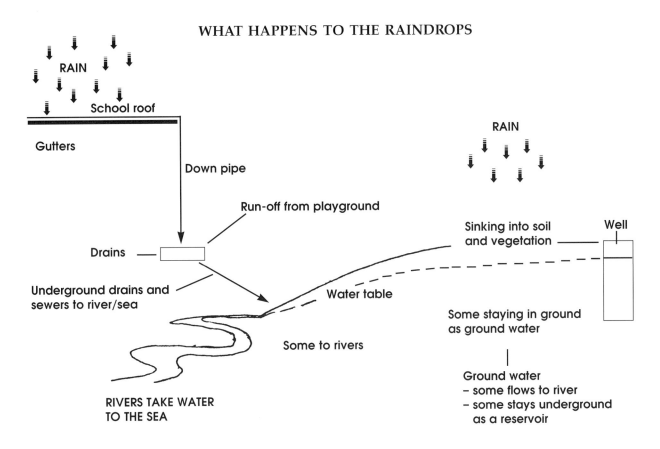

RAIN

School roof

Gutters

Down pipe

Run-off from playground

Drains

Underground drains and sewers to river/sea

Water table

Some to rivers

RIVERS TAKE WATER TO THE SEA

RAIN

Sinking into soil and vegetation

Well

Some staying in ground as ground water

Ground water
– some flows to river
– some stays underground as a reservoir

- draw arrows to show the direction of flow of the surface run-off.

Help the children to work out, by looking at the slope of the land, which way the underground drains are likely to flow. Use the position of any manhole covers to check this.

Look at local maps to see if there are any streams or rivers nearby to take the overflow. Are there any streams on the site? Have any ponds been built to make the most of the rainfall run-off?

LOOKING AT WATER FLOW

The flow of water over the surface can also be studied by using models. Even at Key Stage 1, sandpits and stream flow tanks can be used for experimenting with water flow to see how the landscape can be shaped by running water. The school site may also provide opportunities for creating channels to encourage water flow into and through ponds and this will show how ponds silt up and allow different habitats to develop. Some school sites may be suitable for building small streams. Another possibility is to run a hosepipe (though not in times of drought!) to show where water can flow and collect in puddles.

HOW QUICKLY DOES THE WATER SOAK AWAY?

For schools considering the creation of a new pond, the children could be engaged in a number of activities that will help to select the best site. Although access and health and safety issues will be paramount, the

A stream constructed in the school grounds

slope of the land and the permeability of the soil will also be key factors. This activity shows how to test for permeability.

You will need:
- a hand trowel;
- a cylinder for containing water (a cut-off plastic lemonade bottle would be suitable);
- a simple stop watch.

Use the hand trowel to cut and fold back a small area of turf (about the size of this page). Ease the cylinder into the top 2–3 cm of exposed soil so that a measured amount (1 litre) of water can be carefully poured in. With the stop watch measure the amount of time the water takes to soak into the soil. When you have finished, carefully replace the turf and firm it down.

This activity can be carried out in different parts of the school grounds. Each site will need to be numbered and located on a plan so that a permeability map can be plotted.

Such a map may be useful when planning the location of a school pond or when planting out areas with different vegetation.

How quickly does the water soak away?

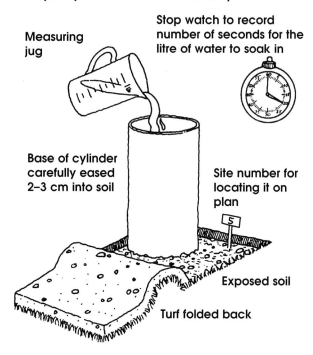

Measuring jug

Stop watch to record number of seconds for the litre of water to soak in

Base of cylinder carefully eased 2–3 cm into soil

Site number for locating it on plan

Exposed soil

Turf folded back

PUDDLE TROUBLE

A variation of the previous activity could be developed for a tarmac playground surface.
- Where do puddles develop?
  This is easily marked out by tracing the puddles with chalk.

- Why do puddles form in certain locations? On what ground surfaces do puddles form?
- How long do the puddles last? Chalk outlines could be drawn at 15 minute intervals to show the puddles shrinking.
- How do the puddles affect our use of the playground?
  Observations will show who avoids the puddles and who enjoys splashing through them.
- How can we get rid of puddles?

Landforms and the school site

It is important to encourage children's awareness of landform so that they learn to recognize the nature of the landscape. However, many schools have only limited variety of landform on their site, so the most needs to be made of what exists. Even an apparently flat landscape may have subtle variations and, in any case, flat land is one form of land shape. How does the landform affect human activity? (For example, are there difficulties for a child in a wheelchair?)

It may be possible to create different landforms around the site. This could be done in a small 'model landscape' area using bucket and spade, or it might be part of a much grander reshaping of part of the grounds – perhaps with the help of a parent or friend of the school with access to a mechanical excavator! Key Stage 1 children may like to create their own landscapes in a sandpit area.

WORD MAPPING
Children can use language to map the school site. Key words can be chosen to describe the local relief. Basic terms such as 'slope' ('gradient' with older children), 'ups and downs' ('topography' with older children), 'hill', 'valley', 'flat', 'steep', 'uneven' can all be introduced and the children can experiment with ways of writing them.

Children at Key Stage 1 could go round the grounds with chalk and/or labelled cards and mark out the different types of landforms. Key Stage 2 children could write appropriate key words over maps of the site. They could work in small groups to produce their own word maps and then compare them with other groups. Some examples of words to describe the grounds are shown in the box below; they could be used to make up a school grounds dictionary.

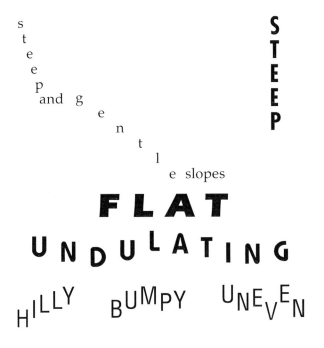

s
t
e
e
p
  and g
        e
          n
            t
              l
                e slopes

**S
T
E
E
P**

F L A T

U N D U L A T I N G

HI**LLY** **B**U**M**P**Y** **U**N**E**V**E**N

Key words to describe the school grounds

Red-brick school building
Temporary huts
Flat playground
Weather-recording station
Narrow steep bank around the edge
Bumpy, hillocky nature area
Sloping games area
Bank beside stream
Trees, bushes, overgrown

USING THE LAND SHAPES

The shape of the land affects our use of it.

- Which parts of the school site are more fun to be in?
- What parts of the site are best for skateboarding or playing marbles?
- What makes a place a 'fun area'? When does a 'fun area' become a dangerous one?

Children could map use in relation to landform, or they could paint/chalk appropriate words or pictures on the playground surfaces.

CONTOURING

Contours are lines that join up places of the same height. They are fundamental to a proper understanding of maps and plans, but difficult for pupils to grasp because they are abstract. One idea would be to draw them with string or ribbon or even get them 'white-lined' on the field. Older children can

do this using ranging poles and simple clinometers. They should line up the poles along land of the same height and then peg out the string to show the contour. The process is as follows:

Pupil A looks through the clinometer and lines up on the two poles.

Pupil B ensures that the clinometer is on the level.

Pupil C moves the second pole up or down the slope until it is at the right height.

Pupils D and E mark the position of the poles and peg out the string accurately.

Ask the children for comments on the finished pattern of contour lines. Are there any patterns emerging from the finished plots? (Where the string is closer, the slope is steeper and vice versa.) Why are the slopes steeper in some areas? Is it to do with the underlying rock type? Has a stream eroded a small valley? Was the earth moved by bulldozers when the school was built?

To make a more permanent record of the contours, children could build a model of the site.

LOOKING OUT AT OTHER LANDFORMS

What are the surrounding landscapes like? The study of landforms can be extended by looking out from the school site. Begin by choosing a range of places that will provide good viewpoints. (See 'Creating a toposcope' on page 18.) Key Stage 2 pupils could be asked the following questions:

- Is the school at roughly the same height as surrounding areas – on a plain or a plateau? Is it higher – on a hilltop? Is it lower – in a valley?
- How steep are the surrounding slopes? Which children walk up or down a steep hill on their way to/from school?
- How far can you see? What are the distances to key features such as hill tops, church towers, chimneys, aerials?
- What words can be used to describe the surrounding areas?

Old maps or documents from the County or District Planning Office may provide some information on what the site was like before the school was built. You could invite a planner in to talk to the children, or there may be parents, ex-pupils or neighbours who knew the site before it was developed.

How the Weather Affects Me

Join each of the sentences to the box which best shows how you feel. One example has been done for you.

When it is hot ...

When it is cold ...

I often feel quite lazy.

I eat more food.

I feel miserable.

I look forward to it snowing.

I stay in and read or watch TV.

My bike gets dirty very quickly.

I don't wear a coat to school.

I enjoy playing outside.

I run home quickly.

I feel happy.

I can't think very well.

I have to wipe my feet.

I like to wear a hat.

I sit on the bench in the playground.

I like playing in the field.

When it is wet ...

When it is dry ...

Can you add any other sentences?

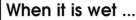

People, Settlements and Land Uses

The school grounds provide a microcosm of the world in a number of ways and can be used to help children develop their understanding of many basic concepts of human geography.

Investigating the school community

The school community mirrors the outside world, even though it is predominantly youthful. By including parents, governors, staff, friends of the school and the range of outsiders who provide services to the school and visit the staff and pupils within, it soon becomes possible to consider the school as a sample of the local community. Concepts such as population size, structure, distribution, change and migration can all begin to be understood from the experiences that the pupils gain from the school site.

WHO WORKS IN OUR SCHOOL?

Key Stage 1 children can find out who works at the school. Who works indoors? Who works outdoors? What jobs do they do? What do they like and dislike about their jobs?

You could use the diagram on page 32 as the basis for this activity. By identifying which parts of the school site the people usually work in, the spatial pattern of people around the site can be developed. The diagram illustrates one way of showing this.

First the children can 'brainstorm' all the people they think may work at the school. Then check this with different teachers, the secretary and other relevant people. Even a small school will have many people involved. Make a database of people and their jobs.

Are there any stereotypes to challenge? Some preparation will be needed to help children look at appropriate questions. Is the caretaker male? Is the cleaner female? Are the bus/delivery drivers male? Are people from different ethnic groups involved with

work at the school? Does the school encourage older people from the community to come in? When parents support the school, do the dads help with reading and the mums with sports or making equipment or digging flower beds for the school?

Once the people are identified the children can decide what questions they want to ask. It is better to get them to agree on the basic questions at least. Help them to see that questions like 'How long does it take you to get to school?' are less intrusive than 'Where do you live?'.

The children should consider how and when they are going to interview their particular person. It will be better if they work in pairs, with one pupil asking the questions and the other recording the answers, either by tape recording or by writing. They could also report back to the class through a series of little plays: 'When I interviewed Mrs X'.

PROFILING OUR COMMUNITY

At Key Stage 2 the children could try to find out how similar the school community is to the local community. They will need to collect data on both the children and the adults who work in the school. The box on page 33 suggests some ways that this information could be displayed.

Census information could be obtained from the local council or collected by the pupils: 'In the five houses nearest to me there are ... (numbers of adults and children, age/sex of children, occupations of adults)'.

The children could construct questionnaires, using a word processing program or a database such as Junior Pinpoint, to find out about the school's neighbours, parents and visitors. Questions could be included about the jobs people do and where they work. With older children some classification of different types of jobs could be attempted.

The next task is to try to make some sense of all the information that is collected. Why do some people work in one type of job in this area? Why do some people travel a long

WHO WORKS IN OUR SCHOOL?

M _____
the contractor who cuts the grass

____ job is _____

____ works from _____ to _____

Children in Year 2
(We work here too!)

_____ Mrs Jones _____
the Year 1 class teacher

Her job is teaching

She works from 8·30 to 5 p.m.

M _____
the Year 2 class teacher

____ job is _____

____ works from _____ to _____

M _____
the classroom assistant

____ job is _____

____ works from _____ to _____

M _____
the headteacher

____ job is _____

____ works from _____ to _____

M _____
the canteen manager

__ job is _____

__ works from _____ to _____

M _____
the cleaner

__ job is _____

__ works from _____ to _____

M _____
the caretaker

__ job is _____

__ works from _____ to _____

M _____
the mealtime assistant/
playground supervisor

__ job is _____

__ works from _____ to _____

M _____
the school secretary

____ job is _____

____ works from _____ to _____

M _____
the school bus driver

__ job is _____

__ works from _____ to _____

M _____
the lollipop man/lady

__ job is _____

__ works from _____ to _____

M _____
the delivery driver

____ job is _____

____ works from _____ to _____

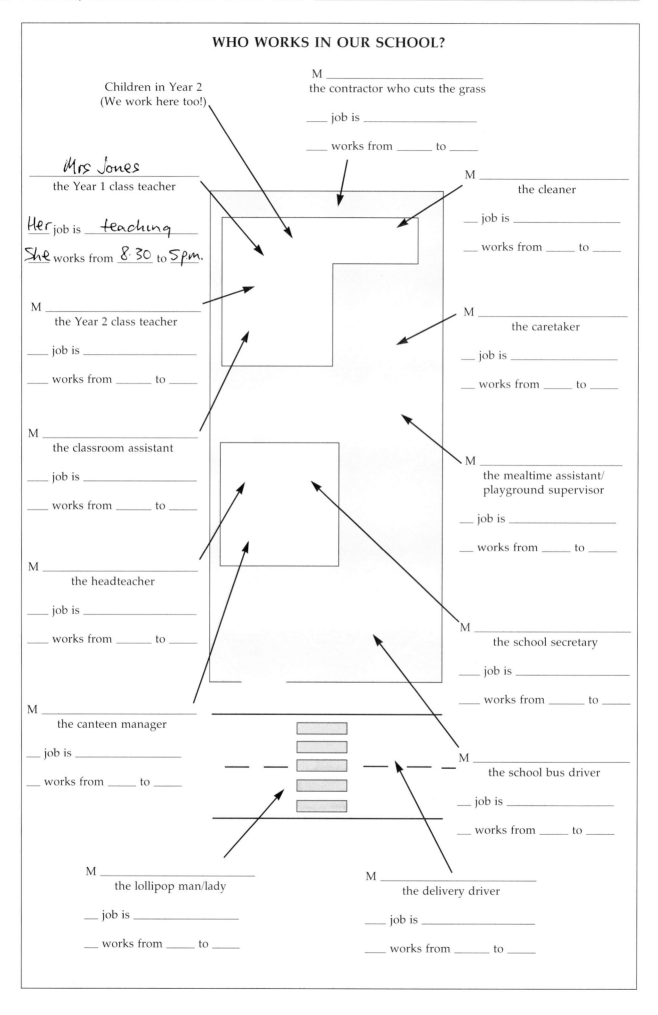

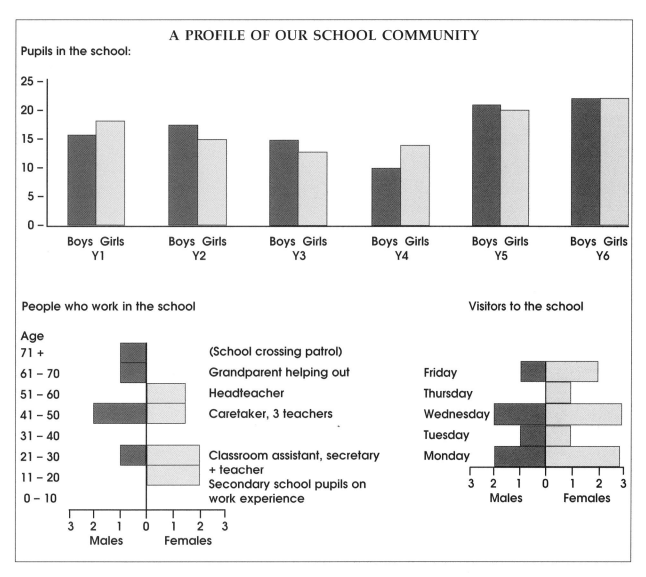

A PROFILE OF OUR SCHOOL COMMUNITY

Pupils in the school:

People who work in the school

Age
71 +	(School crossing patrol)
61 – 70	Grandparent helping out
51 – 60	Headteacher
41 – 50	Caretaker, 3 teachers
31 – 40	
21 – 30	Classroom assistant, secretary + teacher
11 – 20	Secondary school pupils on work experience
0 – 10	

3 2 1 0 1 2 3
Males Females

Visitors to the school

Friday
Thursday
Wednesday
Tuesday
Monday

3 2 1 0 1 2 3
Males Females

way to work? Why do some jobs seem to employ more men than women and vice versa? Why are more and more people moving to (or away from) the local area?

A RECORD OF EACH CHILD

By making a record of themselves, children can identify their part in the school community. Children in Year 1 could make a mural of their hand prints. This could be done in paint on the playground wall (rubber gloves will be needed if gloss paint is used), in wet concrete or on a clay tile which could be baked in a kiln. Children in Year 3 could paint a picture of themselves as they move from Infants to Juniors.

Children can paint their portraits on a wall as part of their school record.

Each child could have a section of a wall to identify themselves over their time in school: 'my first piece of work', 'my height at end of Year 3, Year 4, etc.', 'my favourite piece of work', and so on. A whole area could be given over to displaying a tile for every child who leaves the school.

MOVING AROUND THE SCHOOL

Make a large but simple plan of the school with classrooms, corridors and common areas marked on as well as the main areas of the school grounds. Mount it on card and cover it with clear plastic.

Regularly talk to Key Stage 1 children about where they are going to move to during the day and how they will get there. Mark the route on the plan in pen, e.g. from classroom to playground for playtime. 'Do we turn left or right out of the classroom?' 'Which classrooms do we pass on the way?'

As children become more experienced they can take it in turns to mark on the route and describe it to the others. Their class's route to the playground could be compared with that of other classes using different colour lines. This may promote discussion about where congestion occurs, how well used, or underused, certain paths and doors are. Can the children suggest any solutions to the movement problems they have seen?

At certain times of the school day there are very different traffic flows around the site. This includes vehicular traffic to, from and within the site, as well as the movement of people. The box below suggests two starting points for enquiries about the flow of traffic and people, suitable for Key Stage 2. A map focusing on the adjacent roads and vehicular entrances, car parking areas, bike sheds and unloading areas is needed for the vehicle flows. For the people flows prepare a distorted map, clearly showing the places that people move to/from and the corridors and pathways that are available.

At the beginning of the enquiry ask the children to think about the flows and patterns that they might expect to find. This may identify some central ideas that could be tested, for example:

- the school generates a traffic problem only at the beginning and end of the school day;
- traffic coming on to the school site presents a possible danger to pupils;
- wet playtimes make some of the corridors dangerous for the infants;
- a one-way system in some parts of the school would ease the movement of pupils at busy periods of the day.

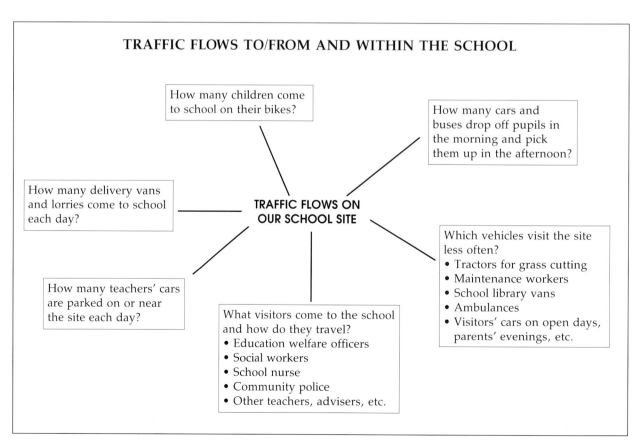

TRAFFIC FLOWS TO/FROM AND WITHIN THE SCHOOL

How many children come to school on their bikes?

How many cars and buses drop off pupils in the morning and pick them up in the afternoon?

How many delivery vans and lorries come to school each day?

TRAFFIC FLOWS ON OUR SCHOOL SITE

Which vehicles visit the site less often?
- Tractors for grass cutting
- Maintenance workers
- School library vans
- Ambulances
- Visitors' cars on open days, parents' evenings, etc.

How many teachers' cars are parked on or near the site each day?

What visitors come to the school and how do they travel?
- Education welfare officers
- Social workers
- School nurse
- Community police
- Other teachers, advisers, etc.

A study of the different uses of the site will reveal which parts are most popular for play.

THE THINGS PEOPLE DO

Various groups of people use different parts of the school site for many different purposes. Some of these will be known to the children, others less so. Some can be observed and recorded at first hand but others will require further research, including the use of interviewing skills and the reviewing of evidence. The diagram at the top of page 36 shows some of the activities that might occur within the school's boundaries during the course of a year.

How do the children feel about their school being used in these ways? Key Stage 2 children could see if there is evidence that any of these activities cause problems to the school. What is the extent of the problem? Can they suggest any solutions to reduce or overcome the difficulties? What action can be taken?

Considerable thought needs to be given to how the children will collect their data:

- Can children living very close to the school collect data before the school day starts and after it has ended?
- Will it be possible to organize a rota so that pairs of pupils can record for two different 15 minute time slots during the school day?
- Where can the children record from? Two chairs placed in an entrance hall should enable them to see what is happening clearly, as long as they don't block route ways and become a traffic hazard themselves!

A standard recording sheet will be needed. The children will need to record information for regular time slots, be able to agree, for example, on the difference between a van and a lorry, and be able to count and record clearly. Pedometers or calculators could be used to record pupil movements at busy periods.

Use I.T. to present the data since this will make any calculating much easier and will produce good quality graphics and word processed reports.

Analyse the evidence collected in the context of the central idea to be tested. This helps the children to focus their ideas. If there is a real issue of concern to the school then the pupils could produce a report for presentation to an audience, perhaps as part of a school assembly, or during an open day or to a meeting of the governing body.

WHERE DO WE PLAY?

Studying the problems of play can develop the children's spatial awareness and lead to some real problem solving and conflict resolution. All individuals and groups play in different ways and their activities and games may have very different spatial requirements. This activity could be used in Key Stage 1 or developed more thoroughly for older children.

Ask each child, or group of children, which parts of the site they enjoy being in and which areas they dislike or tend not to use. Let them think about this outside. Their answers could be plotted on overhead projector transparencies and used to build up an overall picture of favoured and disliked areas. The illustrations overleaf show one way of doing this.

Are there particular areas where conflicts often occur? Help the children to identify any problem areas and try to suggest solutions.

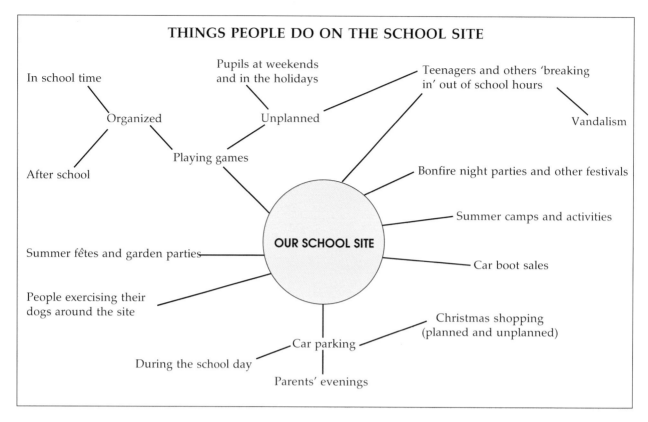

THINGS PEOPLE DO ON THE SCHOOL SITE

Should part of the playground be a football-free zone or non-running area? Should the teachers' cars be parked elsewhere? Can access to parts of the site be improved for use during and immediately after wet weather? Can certain areas be designated for particular activities, such as skipping, marbles, playing with hoops or toy cars or by building a climbing frame there? Are flat or sloping areas better for some activities than others?

KEEPING THE SCHOOL TIDY
Litter is a problem on most school sites. Usually it is fairly obvious where the litter comes from, but why does it collect in certain

Each child can produce an overlay for a plan of the site, to show areas that are liked and disliked.

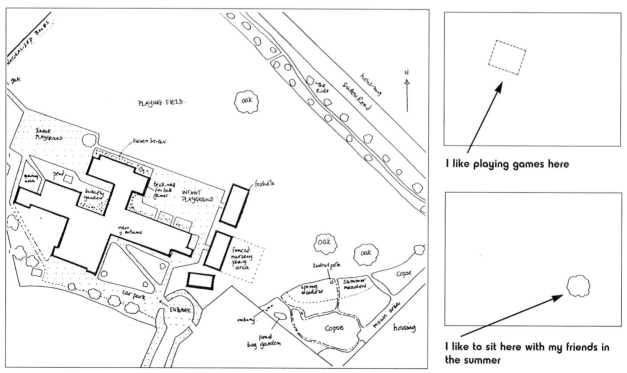

I like playing games here

I like to sit here with my friends in the summer

Top left: Planning a maze
can involve the children.

Above: A multicoloured
maze can be adapted to
all sorts of activities.

Above: This maze is based on an Islamic design,
providing a multi-cultural aspect in the grounds.

Right: Wooden palings have been used to make
this maze which has proved popular for games
and curriculum work.

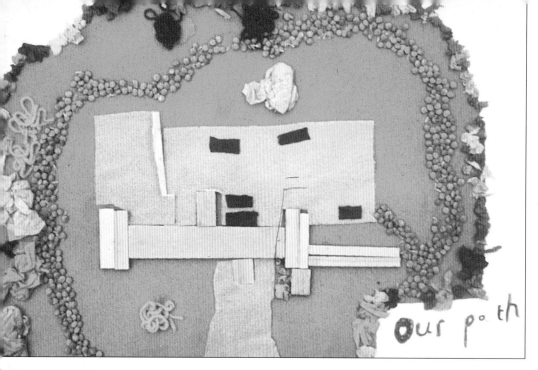

◄ Making a collage of their school helps children to visualize their surroundings.

◄ A collage is also an effective way of recording land use on the site.

◄ A world map painted on a wall is useful in learning about distant places.

At Lipson Vale Primary School ➤ in Plymouth, the Ordnance Survey map has been used as the basis for work with aerial photos and land-use mapping.

Superplan...

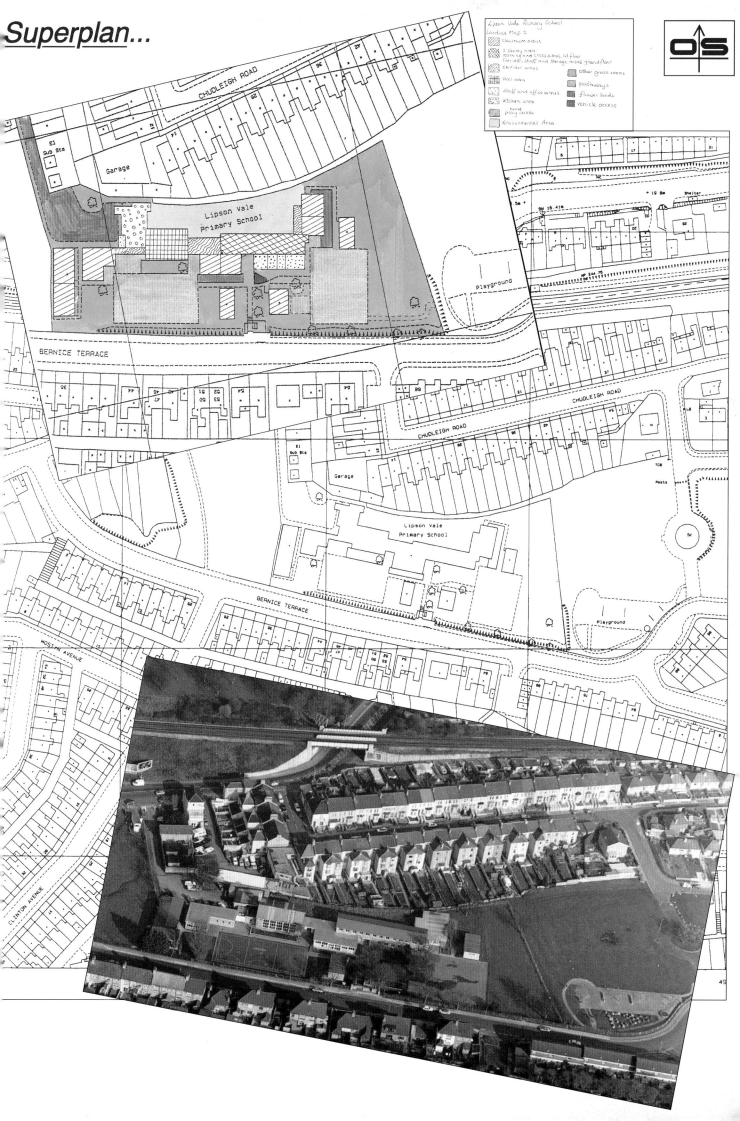

Left: Creating a wildlife garden helps to increase the children's understanding of ecology.

Below: A compass painted on the playground is useful for learning mapping skills.

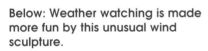

Below: Weather watching is made more fun by this unusual wind sculpture.

Below right: Coloured footprints can be designed to make interesting direction signs.

places and what can be done about it? This enquiry is suitable for Key Stage 1 or could be developed further for Key Stage 2. (Children need protective gloves if they are handling litter of any kind and will need to be reminded of the dangers of finding needles and syringes.)

Working in twos or threes, the children should record the types of litter found – plastics, paper, cardboard, cans (steel and aluminium), textiles, etc. They should also record the location of the different items of litter. This may vary from day to day according to weather conditions and wind direction.

Once all the information is collected the results can be displayed. The children will then be able to formulate some questions:

- Are some classes more guilty of dropping litter than others?
- Is a proportion of the litter dropped by visitors or blown on to the site from elsewhere?
- Are there enough litter bins and are they sited in the best places?
- Should the school have its own recycling skips for paper and/or cans?

They could also be asked to think about:
- Should we look for returnable drinks containers when we go shopping?
- Can we design windbreaks to capture the litter before it blows into more public areas?
- Why do we try to recycle more of our waste?

Settlements

A settlement is any form of human habitation, from a single house to a large city. The school forms part of a settlement: it may be a focal point in a rural village, an anonymous part of a sprawling suburb or a thriving urban community centre. By looking at the school site in the context of the local community, children will be helped to develop an understanding of their locality.

At Key Stage 1 the school and the home are the obvious starting points for children to begin to explore their world. A better understanding of their own locality will help them to appreciate and understand more distant places. The software package 'Number 62 Honeypot Lane' provides a series of investigations for children to learn more about where they live and how they can explore their own environment.

SKYLINES SEEN FROM THE SCHOOL GROUNDS
Silhouettes of the local skylines can be easily produced from photographs. From a good vantage point within the building or grounds take a series of photographs sweeping 360° around the whole of the perimeter. (If you have taken photographs to use with 'Creating a toposcope' on page 18, you may be able to use some of them here.) Cut off the sky and trace round the silhouettes on black card or sugar paper. These can be used in many ways:
- Silhouettes can be used to help children identify different types of housing, office blocks, factories and other features.
- If the photographs have been carefully taken so that they join up to each other consecutively (easier with a tripod!) then the silhouettes can be assembled to make a panorama. You could cut the silhouettes (or the whole panorama) into sections, mix them up and then ask the children to reassemble them to match the skyline. This will help in the development of observation skills.
- A set of photos can be taken from the same spot every four or five years to build up a record of change in the local area.

Key Stage 2 pupils can make their own 'skyline pictures' in the form of a collage, using photos, their own drawings and paintings, and textiles and other materials. A video or ION camera could also be used to produce a 'skyline'. Older children will notice such things as TV aerials, satellite dishes, overhead wires, smoking chimneys, different types of trees, pylons and masts. Some examples of annotated skylines are shown in the illustration on page 38.

FINDING OUT ABOUT THE LOCAL ENVIRONMENT
The skylines can be used as starting points for further work. Identify different categories of buildings and investigate their use. Link this with learning about different people and their jobs: visitors from the surrounding buildings could talk about who they are and what they do.

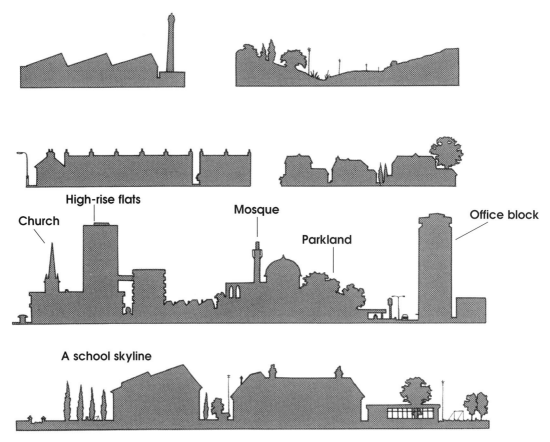

Some examples of skyline silhouettes that might be seen from vantage points in the school

At Key Stage 2, ask the children to locate the features they have drawn on their sky-lines on a local map. How far away are they? To what extent does the relief of the surrounding land open up or cut off views?

Children could shade in the areas that they can see, either on a large-scale map or a small-scale plan. On a plan, this may mean not colouring in the areas behind buildings or trees.

Use these maps to identify some of the other buildings in the local environment that are important to the children:
- a local supermarket or other shops;
- community centres, health centres, play schools/nurseries;
- places of worship;
- parks, recreation grounds, swimming pools, sports centres.

SKETCHING THE LANDSCAPE
Children will find this easier if the view they are sketching is restricted. Cut out some cardboard frames and ask the children to draw just the area that can be seen through the frame; this will help them to focus on a manageable space. From their viewpoint children can be asked to:
- choose a particular feature or group of

buildings to focus on, and begin by drawing an outline shape;
- add detail to their outline (What are the

Sketching a view develops observational skills

features that suggest the building is a factory, office block, modern house, etc.?);

- add labels to their drawings to show that they have been able to identify such features as loading bays, conservatories and architectural details;
- explain how they think the details they have drawn relate to the function of the building (Why do office blocks have large windows, shops have display areas or burglar alarms, houses have porches built on?).

THE CHANGING SITE

Some schools are a product of growth over time, with buildings added bit by bit. Sometimes the extent of the school grounds has been increased, but more commonly buildings have been added to the existing site. Investigations can help children to understand the impact of change as well as some of the reasons behind it, all of which adds to an understanding of the local community. Documentary evidence may be available from the school's log book or the County Education Office. The original building plans may still be available for some schools. Recently revised copies of Ordnance Survey maps of 1832–3 are available also.

Why here?

Why was the school built on this site? Documentary evidence may pinpoint particular reasons but two general factors will determine location – the need for a school to serve a local population and the availability of a relatively large, level site. At Key Stage 1, look at the school's catchment area. How far away are the neighbouring infant/junior/primary/middle schools? How easy is it to travel from one to another? Where do the pupils in the class live? (Usually this can easily be plotted on a local map.)

At Key Stage 2, go on to ask how appropriate the site is for a school. Children could investigate this in a number of ways:

- How good are the local roads?
- Are the footpaths to and from the school safe?
- Has traffic increased since the school was first built?
- How level is the school site? What evidence is there that earth-moving equipment was used to level any part of the site?
- How have the steeper or less accessible

parts of the site been used? Are there any opportunities for developing these areas?

How has the site changed?

Some local people may remember the area before the school was built or may have been pupils at the school in the past. Parents, grandparents and others can be invited to return to the school and recall their memories. This may best be researched through a structured interview. Begin with a brainstorm with the whole class (some ideas are shown in the box below) and then ask them to think about a logical sequence of questioning that will make the visitor feel welcome and then jog his or her memory in a way that will provide the greatest insights. The interview could be conducted as a trail around the grounds and buildings.

Older children will also be capable of making detailed observations about changes made to the fabric of the school. The box on page 40 illustrates some of the changes that may have occurred.

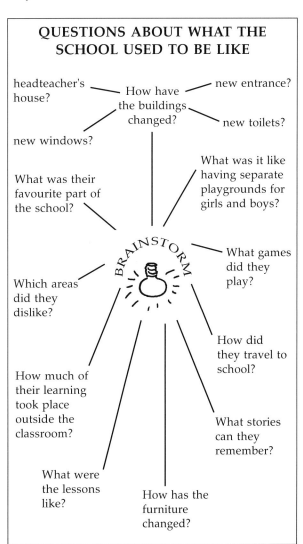

QUESTIONS ABOUT WHAT THE SCHOOL USED TO BE LIKE

headteacher's house?

How have the buildings changed?

new entrance?

new toilets?

new windows?

What was it like having separate playgrounds for girls and boys?

What was their favourite part of the school?

BRAINSTORM

What games did they play?

Which areas did they dislike?

How did they travel to school?

How much of their learning took place outside the classroom?

What stories can they remember?

What were the lessons like?

How has the furniture changed?

CHANGES TO THE SCHOOL BUILDINGS

(a) A timeline

1890s	1940s/50s	1960s/70s	1990s
Older			Newer
Slate roofs and local stone (smaller, rural schools) Red brick (larger, urban schools) High, tall windows Fancy brickwork	Tiled roofs Wider range of building materials More regular, uniform style	Flat roofs Concrete buildings Rows of large windows Boring designs	More conservation-oriented: smaller windows double-glazed greater use of plastics Often more imaginatively designed

(b) The huts

Concrete-framed
Gable roofs
Rows of windows

➡️

Timber-framed
Gable roofs
Rows of windows

➡️

Wooden panels
Flat roofs
Fewer windows
'Portacabins'

(c) Spot the changes!

- Windows blocked up and/or altered
- Extensions: offices, porches, toilet blocks, etc.
- Replacement doors and windows fitted
- Headteacher's/caretaker's house incorporated into main school
- School grounds developed through tree planting, wildlife areas, nature corners, rockeries, picnic areas, safe play areas, etc.

A history trail

The children could develop a history trail and could design their own commemorative plaques to say something about the history of the buildings and the grounds.

On either the inside or the outside of the buildings descriptive plaques could be permanently displayed to provide information on when and why architectural changes were made. They could also be placed at sites that former pupils particularly enjoyed and remembered.

Numbered tiles could be placed at specific points around the site. These could be linked to an audio tape which would lead the visitor around the numbered points and outline the site's development.

Architectural features may reveal the age of different parts of the school

Keyboard overlays could be prepared so that the site could be explored at different levels of difficulty or for different purposes. These could be aimed at Year 3 pupils as they move up to the junior part of the school or new pupils who arrive midway through the school year.

Looking ahead

Children can use the information they have discovered about the school's past to look more critically at the present site. How effective is the design and layout of the school now? What improvements can be made to the buildings and the grounds that will make the whole site a better learning environment?

Car parking

At either key stage children can investigate car parking. How many cars is the school car park designed for? What provision is there for parents and other visitors? Should more or less of the limited amount of space around the school be developed for parking? How can the bringing and collection of pupils by car be made more safe? (What are the views of the local road safety officers and the crossing patrol person?) Where do parents pick up their children or gather in the mornings and afternoons? Is the space well designed? How could it be improved?

Land use

The whole school site is used for a wide variety of purposes and studying these can help children understand some of the principles behind the way that land is used. These include:

- Access – how easy it is to reach an area and make use of it.
- Cost – flat land is much cheaper to build on.
- Appropriateness – flat areas are needed for most sports, sloping areas can make good rockeries or wildscape areas.
- Environmental considerations – some developments (e.g. trees) will enhance the whole site, but others (e.g. a satellite receiving dish) may have a more negative impact.

Sometimes land is used in such a way that makes any subsequent development very restricted. For instance, a Victorian head-teacher's house has small rooms that could be converted into offices but are not suitable for classrooms. Other areas may be more flexible: for example, a hall can be used for assemblies, as a dining area, for drama and P.E., for parents meetings, team teaching, and so on. Outdoors, hard surfaced areas may be suitable for a variety of games (both at playtime and as part of the curriculum), car parking or storage of large items.

PLOTTING LAND USE ON A MAP OF THE SCHOOL SITE

A brainstorm with the pupils will identify a wide range of land uses on the school site. These can then be fitted into categories so that patterns can be identified. For mapping purposes, you will need to agree on a common set of symbols or colours. Some ideas are shown in the box on page 42.

An example of a school's use of a large scale Ordnance Survey map can be seen on the centre pages.

A land-use base map can be used in many ways at either key stage.

1. Calculations can be made to discover the proportion of land given to each type of use.

2. A 3D map can be made to show the intensity of land use, by overlaying the base map with a record of how frequently each part of the site is used. Another method of showing this is to build a model with coloured bricks or use a computer graphics program which can turn a model around so that it can be examined from different aspects.

3. A 3D model can be used to consider over-use and under-use. Is the best use being made of the school site?

4. A range of problem-solving activities can be focused on the map. For example:
- Where else can cars be parked?
- How do we control the 'football' area at playtime?
- Where is the best place to extend the wildlife garden?
- Where should a temporary classroom be sited?
- Which part of the school could be converted into a new nursery centre, with an adjacent outside play area?

5. Children could also use the map for a series of tracking exercises. For example:
- Which play areas are dominated by girls/boys?

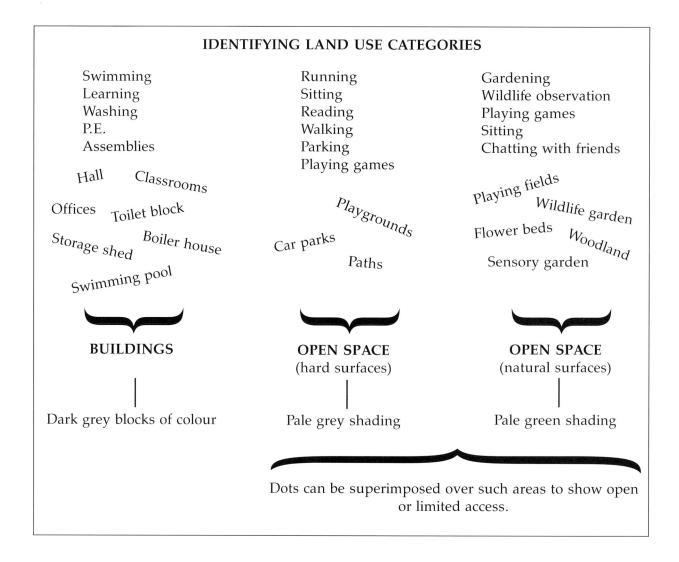

IDENTIFYING LAND USE CATEGORIES

Swimming
Learning
Washing
P.E.
Assemblies

Running
Sitting
Reading
Walking
Parking
Playing games

Gardening
Wildlife observation
Playing games
Sitting
Chatting with friends

Hall   Classrooms

Offices   Toilet block

Storage shed   Boiler house

Swimming pool

Car parks

Playgrounds

Paths

Playing fields

Wildlife garden

Flower beds   Woodland

Sensory garden

BUILDINGS

Dark grey blocks of colour

OPEN SPACE
(hard surfaces)

Pale grey shading

OPEN SPACE
(natural surfaces)

Pale green shading

Dots can be superimposed over such areas to show open or limited access.

- Which parts of the site are most affected by outsiders at weekends and in the holidays?
- Where does the wind-blown litter collect?
- Where should new paths be built or older ones widened?

Any of these ideas could be developed into full investigations which might encourage children to seek solutions for real problems.

WEAR AND TEAR
Some parts of the school site may be over-used and perhaps therefore messy and unattractive. Surfaces may be poorly designed or made from weak materials or damage may be caused simply by too many feet. Particular problems are the spreading path or the playground that overlaps on to grass. Muddy patches, broken paving stones, worn steps, for example, all lower the environmental quality and some may cause potential hazards.

Ask the children to survey the site and find places where the fabric of the buildings or state of the ground appears to show wear and tear. They can record this by video, photographs or on a base map. Ask them to think about the causes so that they identify the issue to be explored or tested.

The second round of observation will be when pupils, visitors or vehicles are moving around the site. Is the damage caused by too many children unable to keep to a narrow path or by a few children behaving badly and ignoring paths or pushing others off them? Is damage caused by vehicles turning or parking in areas where they should be more controlled?

What solutions can the children suggest to reduce the damage and also enhance the site? Help them to think about the advantages and disadvantages of their ideas. Doubling the width of paths is rarely attractive: paving slabs need careful setting, and though gravel is a relatively cheap substitute it is not at all good for wheelchairs. Low fences may prevent vehicles straying on to grass but they can also encourage pupils to sit on them.

Environmental Quality

In simple terms, environmental quality refers to how good or bad, pleasant or unpleasant our surroundings are – in this case the immediate environment of the school site. Whether a person thinks somewhere is nice or nasty depends on their past experience, age, gender, cultural background and so on. It's an individual's judgement because it depends on their perception and interpretation. Children enjoy exploring their senses. Making judgements on the environment can help them recognize their own feelings and values. It helps them shape thoughts and become more sensitive to their own views and more tolerant of other pupils whose collective views may be different from their own.

There are many ways of assessing the environmental quality of the school site, some of which are addressed in the activities in this chapter. Further ideas can be found in other Learning through Landscapes' publications, such as the *Esso Schoolwatch* pack.

What is the environmental quality of the school site?

ARE YOU SMILING?
Even the youngest children can make judgements about attractive and unattractive places around the site. At Key Stage 1 visit a number of places around the school grounds and let the children decide which of three faces to award each site – 'happy', 'O.K.' or 'unhappy'. (See photocopiable page 54.)

The numbers of the different types of faces at each place can then be counted to find out how the whole group feels. Why do some children like particular places? What do they like doing there?

Ask the children to make a bar chart for each place, with three columns – 'happy', 'O.K.' and 'unhappy'. Stick each chart on a map of the school grounds in the right place.

A RAINBOW MAP OF FEELINGS
Older children can use colours to show their feelings about different places. Ask them to

At Heathcoat Primary School part of the site has been reshaped to create a slope.

shade in a map of the school grounds to show how they feel. First discuss with the class which colours go with, say, feeling happy, bored, sad, excited, scared or any other emotions they feel in the school grounds. Then walk around in the grounds and start to make a rainbow map of feelings. The children need to identify the different feelings they experience in different parts of the grounds.

WHY DO WE FEEL THIS WAY?

Ask the children to say what the face or rainbow patterns show and why. Revisit three different places in the grounds that they liked and three that they disliked. Ask them to think very carefully and answer the question: 'Why do you like or dislike each place?' Encourage them to list as many reasons as they can. For example, it might be a fun place but they should say why it is a fun place. If it is dangerous or scary, ask them to say why. Use a chart to record their answers.

Ask the children to compare their reasons with those of their classmates. Make two big lists of everyone's reasons for likes and dislikes.

- Which reasons are found most often?
- Which reasons are caused by people?
- Which reasons are caused by natural things?
- Which reasons could be changed?
- Which reasons could be changed but with some cost?

NICE OR NASTY?

At Key Stage 1, make an environmental profile of a place by using paired and opposite words. Visit a number of places in the grounds and complete a profile in each place. The chart below shows an example of how this can be done. Children can work individually or in pairs.

Using a brightly coloured pen, the children can join up the ticked boxes on each sheet to make a 'profile' for that place. Ask them whether each place is nearer the left-hand side – the 'nice' side – or nearer the right-hand side – the 'nasty' side.

Look at the differences and similarities between different people's profiles. Discuss

---

ENVIRONMENTAL PROFILE

Name of place:_____

For each pair of words, put a tick in the box which you think best describes this place.

Warm	❑	❑	❑	❑	❑	❑	Cold
Nice	❑	❑	❑	❑	❑	❑	Nasty
Quiet	❑	❑	❑	❑	❑	❑	Noisy
Safe	❑	❑	❑	❑	❑	❑	Dangerous
Open	❑	❑	❑	❑	❑	❑	Closed
Friendly	❑	❑	❑	❑	❑	❑	Unfriendly
Colourful	❑	❑	❑	❑	❑	❑	Grey
Light	❑	❑	❑	❑	❑	❑	Dark
Interesting	❑	❑	❑	❑	❑	❑	Boring
Clean	❑	❑	❑	❑	❑	❑	Dirty

The children can identify those parts of the grounds they like, such as a garden and seating area.

place. An average total score for each place is then worked out from the children's scores. The average scores are marked on a map of the school grounds, using either the figures or vertical bars located on each sample place. The patterns can then be described and explained. What are the things that make a place 'nice'? Can the children say how they think the worst places can be improved?

why particular points on the profile between pairs of words have been chosen. Some words, such as 'friendly' and 'ugly', already have positive and negative judgements within them, but others, such as 'noisy', may be more complicated. 'Noisy' might be a more positive word than 'quiet' to some children.

Find out what the pupils think should be done to make 'nasty' places better. Can they see what makes some places 'nice'?

As an extension, try taking some adults to some of these places and ask them to score the places in the same way. Compare the results with the children's views.

At Key Stage 2, the exercise can be quantified by giving each box between the words a score of 1 to 6, with 1 on the good side. An environmental quality map for the school grounds can then be produced. First, each child works out their total score for each

A further refinement is to collect scores at regular intervals, say every 10, 20 or 30 metres across the map, depending on the size of your grounds. A grid drawn on to a large-scale map of the grounds could help pinpoint the sample places. Get the children to produce a colour grading scheme and shade each square according to its score. The shading could grade from light to dark, with 'nice' being light and 'nasty' being dark.

These patterns can be described and explained – say where the nice and nasty places are and suggest reasons why.

A GUIDE TO THE SCHOOL GROUNDS

This can be used to show the environmental quality of the school grounds to visitors or new pupils. Start with a class discussion, to include:

• Why do we need a guide?

Children working on a school guide

Cultural diversity in the school grounds could be celebrated in the children's guide.

• Who is it for?
• What should it show and why?
• How should it look?

The children will need to think carefully about the audience for their guide. It might come from the following list of examples:
• new pupils;
• parents;
• visitors to the school;
• parents and grandparents of pupils who come from an ethnic minority;
• the pupils from a linked primary school elsewhere;
• visually impaired visitors or pupils.

Ask the children to decide what the guide should show. It might include sections on how the grounds have changed, projects in progress or future plans. It could highlight those features made by people and those created by nature. It could emphasize the cultural diversity of the school, showing how the school grounds celebrate this diversity. (The book *People, Plants and Places* may be helpful here, see page 71.) It could trace the historical changes on the site.

Divide the class into groups, with each group allocated a different task. The groups should think hard before starting their work together. They can take responsibility for contributing their part to the whole project. Be sure to find something challenging for each group member to do. Ask them to decide the form their guide could take and how it might be used. They should produce a design and a chart to show the stages of production. The guide could take many forms such as one of the following:
• a folded booklet with a title page, a map to show locations of features and a written commentary;
• a talking guide, drafted first and then dictated on to a tape recorder – it could be made in another language as well as English by a child who speaks that language;
• a large sheet showing a map of the grounds, with a route indicated and written comments and sketches of particular features;
• a concept keyboard overlay;
• a video film produced on a camcorder, in which the children introduce children from another school, perhaps, to the interesting aspects of the grounds.

THE SCHOOL GROUNDS CALENDAR
Ask the children to consider what twelve pictures of the school grounds should be taken for a school calendar. The calendar could feature appropriate pictures for festivals from a variety of faiths – Islam, Hinduism, Christianity – and it could be produced by pupils at either Key Stage 1 or 2.

Think about its purpose and who it is for. It could be produced to help raise funds for future school grounds development. Its audience might be parents, the whole school community or, perhaps the local community.

Ask the children to think about places and landscapes to photograph, and to look at viewpoints and directions. They will need to consider the time of year for each photograph and to write a suitable caption. Inevitably some of the judgements they make will be related to environmental quality.

First steps include either taking sample

shots or producing sketches in a rectangular frame. If you have access to an ION camera (this takes still video pictures that can be seen on a television screen) then a variety of shots can be taken to help with decision making.

These ideas can be used to select views and draw sketches for any similar project, such as producing:
• a school tea towel;
• a greetings card for a festival, such as Divali, Christmas or Thanksgiving;
• a cover for a school recipe book;
• a newsletter for parents;
• a contribution to a local magazine or newspaper.

IS YOUR SITE VISITOR FRIENDLY?

Pupils at Key Stage 1 can invite children from another local school for a visit. Working in pairs, they can show the visitors around the site, then ask them for their reactions and feelings. These can be tape recorded and listened to later. They could ask, for example:
• What things do you like and dislike about our school grounds?
• Where were the best places and why?
• Where were the worst places and why?

At Key Stage 2, adult visitors can be invited and the pupils can prepare questions for them, such as:
• When coming to the school, at what point did you see the school's name on the board outside?
• How did you know which way to go from the front entrance?
• Did you have any difficulties finding your way to the school office or reception? If yes, what were they? If no, then why?
• How welcoming did you find the school from the first moment you stood outside it or drove into the car park?
• Did the feeling of welcome change as you came into the school?
• Did you notice anything particularly pleasant or unpleasant?

If there are any problems, ask the children to suggest a better system for making visitors welcome. They may need to design and perhaps make, new directional signs, suggest images for a new signboard for the school, recommend changes to the reception area, think about how visitors are greeted and/or consider the whole image that the school presents to visitors arriving for the first time.

Ask the children to consider how the school should greet:
• a blind or deaf person;
• a wheelchair user;
• a non-English speaker.

They could either invite appropriate people in to help with this or replicate the experience as closely as possible for themselves, to understand the difficulties the school grounds may present. This might involve planting a sensory garden, producing sound sculptures or wind chimes, improving wheelchair access, or using I.T. to design and produce signs and symbols of welcome.

A WORD IN YOUR EYE

Language activities based on perceptions and descriptions of the school site provide a vocabulary to build a rich word picture of the environment. They help children to observe the environment accurately too.

At Key Stage 1, visit three or four contrasting places in the grounds. Ask the children to write down (or tape record) the words that come into mind in each place. Alternatively, ask them to select from the words on photocopiable page 55. (If there are children in your class who speak other languages, you may wish to add some appropriate words from those languages. Children can also add their own choice of words to the list.) Discuss the words they choose:
• Why were particular words chosen?
• What similarities and differences are there between the pupils' lists?
• What differences are there between words that describe features and those that describe feelings?

Make labels to go on a large wall map of the school grounds and ask the children to stick them in the correct places.

At Key Stage 2, create a word bank or a dictionary of the school grounds in an invented 'foreign' language. Ask the children to walk round the grounds and to list some of the features they find there. They can then invent new words for these features and define the words in English.

Alternatively, children who speak another

Children can draw word pictures to illustrate features in the grounds.

language could provide words in their language with a definition in English. For example, in German, 'baum' is a large plant with a single woody stem, many branches and lots of leaves.

Challenge the children by reading out some of their new words and asking them to recognize the features.

POEMS AND PICTURES

Working in small groups, the children build a list of words for a place they have selected in the grounds. They then use the words to construct a poem related to the place.

Challenge the children to draw pictures with the words they have used to name features in the grounds (like the examples on the right). Where the words describe their feelings about places, ask them to write the words in a way that also expresses their feelings. For instance, can they write words in a style that shows anger about vandalism, or in a style that

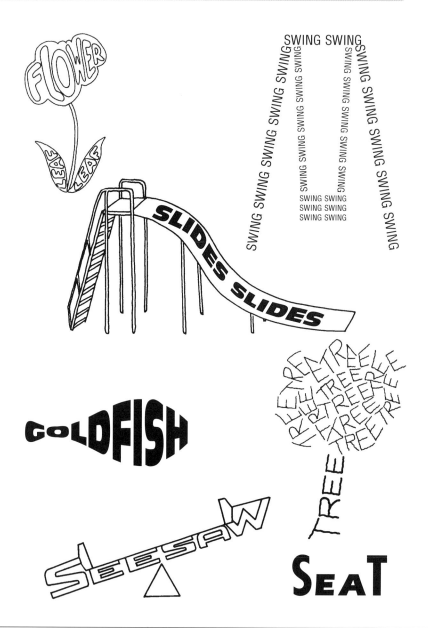

Cross-section of a wildlife garden along a line, A – B

Scale 1:100

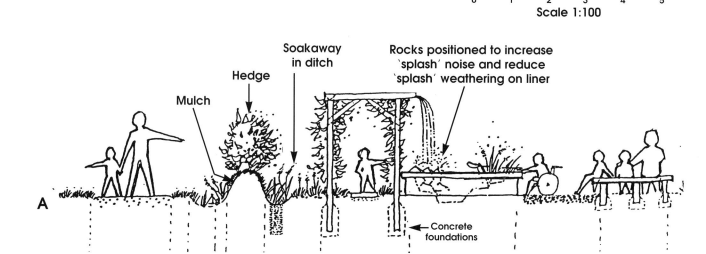

reflects their feelings about a place that makes them feel happy?

PLANTS AND THEIR PLACES

Find out about plants which live in your school grounds and where they come from. Make a list of the plants and use reference materials (or a friendly gardening expert) to research their origins. What kinds of climate and soils do they prefer? Relate this to other work on contrasting localities. Make a guide to plants in the school grounds or a plants trail.

Children can find out the different nationalities and cultures represented in the school. List these on a chart or a computer database. Then locate 'home' countries on an atlas. What plants grow in these countries? Are any of them grown in the school grounds? Are there any others which you could grow? (See Julian Agyeman's book *People, Plants and Places*.)

How can the environmental quality be improved?

The first part of this chapter provides some activities to explore the existing environmental quality of the school grounds. This leads, quite naturally, to thinking about what can be done to improve the environmental quality. This is a particular aspect of the Geography National Curriculum in primary schools.

Planted tubs in the playground make a practical learning resource.

There is an extensive range of sources of advice and case studies to help school communities, including material produced by Learning through Landscapes (see the 'Resources' section at the end of the book). Central to any school grounds development is the involvement of the children at every stage. Changing an environment for the better also involves using geographical skills, knowledge and understanding in a practical way. It follows, then, that children can learn a great deal about geography while helping to improve their own school grounds.

Geographical experiences are particularly relevant at the early stages of thinking about the present site and surveying it. Geography is also important when planning the changes and during evaluation.

IMPROVING THE GROUNDS FOR WILDLIFE

All school grounds can support some wildlife, even if it is only a few insects and some stubborn weeds. Many schools have gone much further in encouraging wildlife by widening the number of habitats and so improving the environment. At the same time, the work involved can help to increase children's understanding of various aspects of ecology, such as habitats, plant and animal associations, and the effect of rainfall, sunshine and shade on plants.

On a large plan of the school grounds, help the children select sample lines across

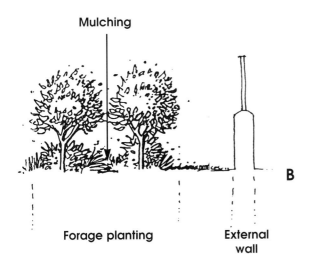

Mulching

Forage planting

External wall

B

Creating a bog habitat will encourage different types of wildlife.

which this project could be tackled is shown in the box below.

The next step is for the children to try to complete the planning sheet. Clearly, some of the action points are difficult to fill in and the children should put in question marks for those which they cannot complete. If the project were to be carried out, then these are precisely the questions that need answering before any practical steps are taken.

the grounds. They should then pace right across the grounds, following their line, as closely as possible.

Next they need to draw on a strip of paper a map of all the features they meet as they cross the grounds. They will need to select a suitable scale, such as 10 paces to 1 centimetre, to get the sketch map approximately right. Sitting to one side of their line, they can try to draw a labelled cross-section, like that shown on page 48, using the sketch map strip as a guide. They may need help to estimate the height of some features and to try to draw them to the same scale.

The children can now try to discover what wildlife is supported along this cross-section. Let small groups of pupils concentrate on particular habitats. Some guidance on studying wildlife in the school grounds can be found in *Science in the School Grounds* in this series.

AN AFRICAN HOUSE

At Key Stage 2, children can be more fully involved in the process of environmental improvement in the school grounds. A planning exercise focused on just one change can help them to think about the whole process.

Ask the children to consider all the steps needed to create in the school grounds a full-scale replica of a family house from a less-well-developed part of Africa. This could be part of a term's work focused on an African locality. Let the children work in small groups and ask them to suggest the stages for the project, using the planning sheet on page 52. An example of one way in

THE STAGES IN BUILDING A TRADITIONAL AFRICAN VILLAGE HOUSE

Stage 1
The pupils want to find out what it is really like to live in a traditional African house, as part of their topic on looking at an African family.

Stage 2
The pupils survey the school site to find a suitable place to build the house. They and the teacher check with the headteacher and the governors that this is a project they will support.

Stage 3
The pupils carry out detailed planning, talking with parents who would like to support the project. They consider the time available, money, materials and space required and safety considerations.

Stage 4
The pupils, together with the teacher and headteacher, consult school neighbours, local builders, the local authority and members of the African community living in the area. They also seek official permission.

Stage 5
Detailed costings are made at this stage in a master plan. Fundraising is started and sponsorship is requested from a local supermarket.

Stage 6
The pupils, teachers and parents work under the supervision of a parent who is a builder to make the walls of mud, strengthened with straw and capped against the rain. A suitable roof is made with corrugated iron.

Stage 7
The pupils hold a grand opening day to celebrate completion, with a drama presentation showing the lives of a family in an African village. Afterwards the pupils judge how successful the whole project has been and put the house to long-term use at playtimes.

PLANNING GEOGRAPHICAL PROJECTS IN THE SCHOOL GROUNDS

The blank planning sheet on page 52 can be photocopied for the children to map out their own steps for planning other projects, such as:

- A mural showing an aerial view of the school and surrounding districts (as in this photograph).
- A distance signpost, like the one at Land's End, which shows the distance and direction from your school to places around the world.
- Re-creating a feature of the local natural environment in your school grounds (see Chapter 3) like the bog shown in the photograph on the previous page, or a landscape of miniature hills and valleys.

- Creating a stream running through the school grounds from one pond to another, making use of rainwater running off roofs (see the photograph on page 27).
- Making a geology rock garden or wall.
- Researching the place names of the local area and of the school site before it was built on and making a set of place name labels for all the features of the site.

Developing your site

It is important to be aware that there are many issues to address, too lengthy to consider here, before undertaking any practical work on your school grounds. Learning through Landscapes' research has shown that the most successful projects are those which follow these three key principles:

- sustainable – involving the use, design, maintenance and management of school grounds;
- holistic – involving the whole site, the whole community and the whole curriculum, i.e. its formal, informal and hidden aspects;
- participative – involving children and adults.

A mural like this uses mapping and artistic skills.

Planning changes in the school grounds

Project title:				
Number and title of stage	Stage of the project	Who can help us with this stage?	How much time might be needed for this stage?	How much might each stage cost?
1. Thinking				
2. Surveying				
3. Planning changes				
4. Talking to people				
5. Costings				
6. Doing it!				
7. Does it work? What mainten-ance is needed?				

GOOD PRACTICE IN THE DEVELOPMENT OF SCHOOL GROUNDS

- Gain agreement from the whole school community, pupils, staff, governors, parents and friends, that the grounds should be developed.

- Ensure that any working group or management team that steers development contains representatives from all parts of the school community.

- Develop a strategy for school grounds development and incorporate it in the school's development plan.

- Make clear the links between school grounds development and all aspects of the curriculum.

- Investigate other schools' achievements.

- Involve children at all stages.

- Have a flexible approach to the evolving grounds.

- Within the plan for the whole site, assess the time needed for each stage and implement the plan in manageable phases.

- Appreciate that the process of change may be more important than the final product.

- Involve a wide range of outside specialists and make good use of expertise within the school community.

A plan of a developed school site: the names chosen for the different parts of the grounds reflect the history of the area.

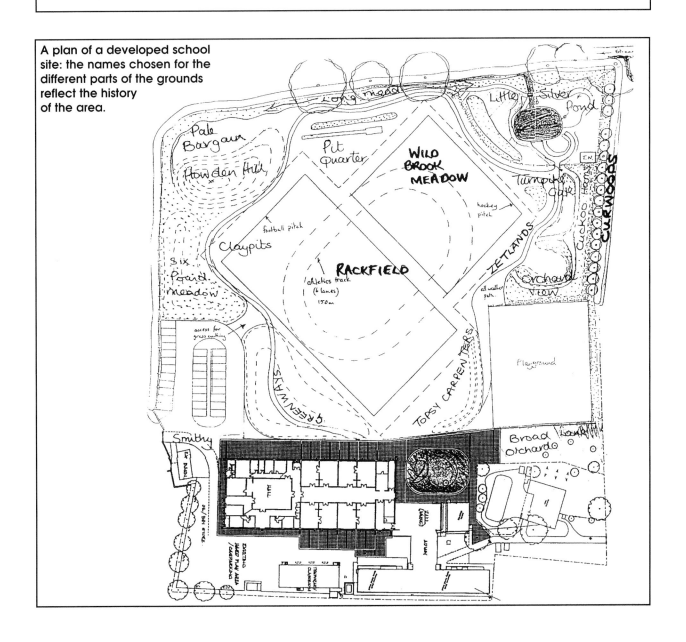

How do places around you make you feel?

Choose ten places. Go to each one in turn. Draw a face to show how you feel at each place.

Happy	O.K.	Unhappy

Place	Face

Words to describe the school grounds

smooth	friendly	unfriendly	rough
flat	quiet	loud	green
interesting	grey	fun	games
boring	secret	play	soft
cold	hard	sandy	wet
grassy	muddy	dry	scary
little	big	closed in	wide open
crowded	new	old	lonely
sad	bare	happy	woody
creepy	cool	high	low

A Sense of Place

What do we mean by a sense of place?

Every place is unique. Pause for a moment and think of the place where you grew up. Can you summon to mind the various landscape features and their distribution? How about the surfaces, textures and colours, the smells and the feel of the place? Now repopulate it with people, events and history and you have a heady mixture of memories, and perhaps nostalgia too. For children to grasp this notion of a sense of place, it may be helpful to start in the school and its grounds.

THROUGH THE KEYHOLE

Help the children at Key Stage 1 to find out the special nature of the different spaces, both inside and outside, that make up the school. Start by presenting them with a series of clues about each place in turn until they guess which space it is. Try to compose descriptive sentences that really bring out the flavour of the place. It could be a particular corner of the playground, a stock cupboard, an office, a flower bed near the road or any other space on your site. Include the smell, sounds and feel of the place as well as describing what is there and what it looks like.

Alternatively, divide the children into small groups and take each group to one particular space. Ask them to find words to describe the features of their space, perhaps using a list like that in the box on page 55 to help them. The children then present their clues to the rest of the class until their space is guessed. You could also ask the children who recognize the description to point to the space on a large map of the school and say why they guessed it.

AND ON YOUR RIGHT ...

At Key Stage 2, children can draw labelled pictures and write a full description of each space, emphasizing its unique features and distinctive flavour. Working in small groups, they should choose a particular style of presentation and produce descriptions of one or two places per group. They might need some examples of descriptive writing to guide them. You could provide extracts from various sources, such as a stately home guide, an estate agent's description of a house or a guide to a local tourist attraction like a restored mill.

The descriptions are then pieced together to make the group's guide to the chosen places around the school.

What makes your school grounds unique?

Even in schools which were built at the same time and to a similar pattern, there are differences in layout, detail, materials and uses.

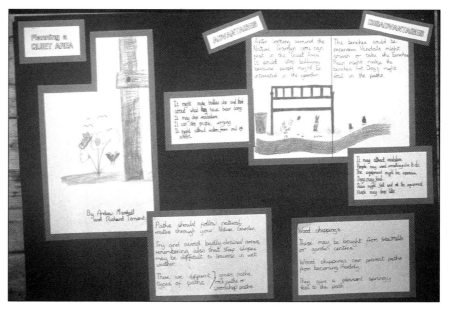

Planning a quiet area in the school grounds encourages careful observation.

CELEBRATING A SPECIAL PLACE

At Key Stage 1, get the children to create a texture map of the school grounds. They can collect samples of all the materials that make up the different areas and place or stick them in the correct places on a map of the site. Ask the children about the other things that make the school grounds special to them.

Key Stage 1 children can also be asked to select one special feature of the grounds which can be incorporated into a design for a celebration flower bed. They could use an art software program to help produce their designs. At Key Stage 2, this activity can be extended by the children using a seed catalogue to suggest the appropriate flowers for the bed, taking note of flower height, preferred soil conditions, cost, flowering times, etc. The natural end point for this activity is to select a site for the flower bed, gain permission for preparing it, acquire funding and then actually make it. Of course, the pupils should be centrally involved at every stage.

At Key Stage 2, encourage the children to produce a collage of photographs of all the features, details and particular aspects that make the grounds special. Ask them to

A welcome board designed by the children

A mosaic on a wall showing a pond habitat

A welcome board in different languages helps to break down cultural barriers.

decide what needs to be photographed and let them take the shots. The collage could be stuck on to a large map of the school or laid out in the shape of the whole school grounds as seen from above.

Again at Key Stage 2, let small groups of children construct mosaics to celebrate the most treasured aspects of the school grounds. These aspects need to be identified and agreed on first and a design created. The mosaic could perhaps incorporate some of the materials from the grounds themselves.

Ask the children to design a new school logo, a flag, a letterhead or a welcome board, like the ones shown in the photographs here, based on some of the distinctive features of the school grounds.

VIRTUAL REALITY WALK

At Key Stage 1, use a large map or, better still, a model of the school grounds. Tell the children to use their fingers to walk from one place to another, following routes suggested by other children. They have to follow the directions as closely as possible. The children setting the routes should use words that indicate direction.

Next they should do the same thing with the child describing the route having his or her back to the map or model. This means that they have to create an image of the grounds in their minds.

At Key Stage 2, tell the pupils to think for a moment of the school grounds. Ask them to close their eyes then to use their memories to take a walk through the grounds. Get them to work in pairs to describe their walks to each other, with the task of identifying the other pupil's start and end points and other features on the walk. Each child could draw on a map the route described by the other as they talk.

OUR ELASTIC SCHOOL

Children of any age can try to draw mental maps of the school grounds. (Some examples are shown on the next page.) Some may need a basic outline to help but there is more interest in starting from a blank sheet. This provides the fun of comparing each other's attempts (including the teacher's mental map, of course!) and also comparing them with a surveyor's map. The important thing, however, is to get the children to analyse their maps carefully. At Key Stage 1, the level of the pupils' drawing skills will have a limiting effect but it is still possible to compare the features included or omitted

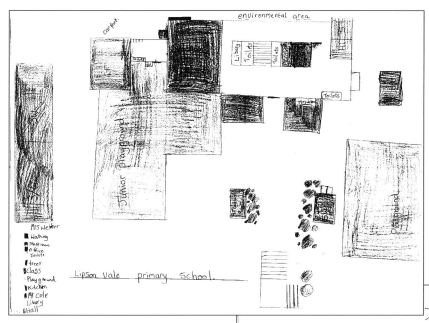

Mental maps of school grounds by Y2 and Y5 pupils, done completely from memory.

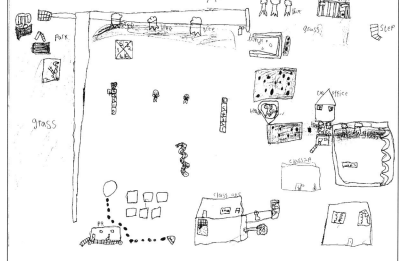

and their relative location. At Key Stage 2, ask the pupils to consider the following questions.

- What distortions are there, comparing their maps with the real map of the grounds?
- What explains the differences between their maps and the surveyor's map?
- Why are some features included and why are some absent?
- What differences are there between the maps drawn by different age groups and why?
- To what extent are differences explained by drawing skills, experience or relative importance of certain features in the children's lives?
- Do the mental maps relate in any way to the pupils' behaviour in the grounds?

MY SPECIAL PLACE

Ask each child in the class to select a small place, which might be only a metre or two across, in the grounds. Every child should choose somewhere separate from other pupils as far as possible. Give them time to get to know their place really well and to focus on the detail that makes the place they have chosen special.

To begin with, they can draw a detailed map of the place, marking in all its minute features. Let them use a hoop or markers to show the boundary of their area on the ground before starting to draw the map.

Each child should pinpoint their special

place on a large map of the school grounds and say why they chose it.

Over the following weeks, the children can adopt their spaces and become 'place guardians'. By making regular visits, they can record their feelings on a tape recorder. They could invite other pupils to their place to show them what is special about it and look at the differences between their individual places. (See *Special Places: Special People.*)

BEATING THE BOUNDS

Many communities still take part in the ancient practice of 'beating the bounds', or 'walking the marches' in Scotland, a ceremonial way of fixing the parish or manorial boundary. You can explore the boundaries of your school grounds in a similar way. (More ideas for activities related to walking the bounds can be found on page 26 of *English in the School Grounds* in this series.)

School boundaries come in many different styles and materials.

In both key stages, try walking around the school boundaries in small groups, with or without a map of the site. Carry out an enquiry into the special nature of the school boundary.

- How long is it? Either count the number of paces of one child and then measure an average stride length, or measure each straight section with a tape measure.
- What different forms does the boundary take (fences, walls, hedges, etc.)? Make a frieze to go around the classroom, showing the different types of boundary. It will need to be drawn to a simple scale where, for example, 1 metre on the boundary is represented by 10 (or 5 or 1) centimetres on the frieze. The lengths of the different types of boundary could be worked out from the frieze, added together and displayed as a horizontal bar chart or pictogram.

At Key Stage 2, pupils can tackle a number of questions that explore issues arising from beating the bounds.

- If there are different types of boundary why is this so? Explain why there might be a high fence around the playground or a low wall somewhere else.
- How does the height of the boundary change and why? The heights of walls and fences can be either measured or estimated, perhaps against the height of a child.
- What are the land uses on either side? Do they affect the nature of the boundary? For example, is there a high fence around an area used for playing football to protect neighbouring gardens? Make drawings to show the land use on either side of the boundary and add them to the frieze.
- How could the boundary be improved? Produce designs for improvements to damaged, old or inappropriate sections of boundary and place them on the frieze.
- Who needs to be involved in any decisions

about the boundary? If there is a need to change the boundary, ask the children to interview someone from the school's governing body to find out if the problem has been identified and what plans there are for change.

- How long has the boundary been there? With old hedgerows it is possible to give a very approximate date by counting the number of woody species of plant over a 30 metre stretch and multiplying by 100. So, for example, if hawthorn, oak and ash trees are found, then the three woody species indicates that the hedge is about 300 years old. Other boundaries may be more difficult to date but there may be clues in the types of materials used or in the boundary's direction.
- Has it changed over the years and if so why? Do any of the boundaries come from the past? Old maps provide many clues, though they may not tell you what the boundaries were made of, only where they were. Write a short history of the school boundary, trying to explain how it has changed over time.

BOUNDARIES – THE HIDDEN MESSAGES

At Key Stage 2, the children can also investigate what the boundaries say about the school.

- Do they appear to be built to keep children in, other people out, or both?
- Are they welcoming and attractive or do they intimidate?
- Do they separate your school from the neighbourhood or link it to it?

Ask the children to produce a report on the boundary for the governors. They can include some of the material gathered earlier and focus on the problem areas and the answers to the questions above, with suggestions for improvement.

FUTURE SHIFTS

Ask the children to investigate whether there are any possibilities for changing the boundaries in the future. Say a plot of land next to the school became vacant when a house, factory or field fell into disuse. If it was bought for school use, how might the boundary be changed to accommodate it? The plot of land might be small – perhaps a triangle of wasteland or a disused garden.

What form of boundary should be created then?

Get the children to use an Ordnance Survey 1:2 500 map to select a suitable plot of land next to the school and to compare the map with the actual landscape. They need to trace on the boundary change and show how the land could be used to help the school.

Ask them to suggest what kind of boundary is needed and why. The pupils can then find out from local builders or fencing contractors about the relative costs of different materials and work out how much it would cost to make the new boundary.

A PLACE BY POST

Ask your pupils at Key Stage 2 to think about the grounds as a whole and take them for a walk around the grounds. Get them to consider how they would describe the grounds to other people. Invite them to send a postcard to a pupil in another school – perhaps one with which your school has a twinning link. They need to draw or photograph the view that best reflects the atmosphere of the school grounds and to write a description in a few sentences that conveys the character of the grounds.

At either key stage the children can design a postage stamp to carry the same message, but this time just visually. They will need to use a large square, rectangular or triangular sheet of paper. The serrated edges of the 'stamp' can be cut with pinking shears. Ensure that they keep the design simple and clear to convey a true sense of the nature of the grounds.

Developing a sense of place

Do your school grounds reflect the place in which they are located? Sometimes the school buildings and grounds have the flavour of the surrounding locality. A small slate-roofed Victorian building with tarmac grounds, clinging to the valley side amongst a row of terraced houses, is not untypical in some of the South Wales valleys. Some schools in the Midlands have flat grassy grounds with the remnants of hawthorn hedgerows around them, reflecting the nature of the surrounding countryside largely shaped by agricultural enclosure. In the modern suburbs of many cities, the new school is built of similar materials to the surrounding semi-detached housing and its landscaped flower beds resemble those in nearby shopping centres.

Identifying this local character and seeing how well the school and its grounds fit together can help children discover more of their local identity and could lead to future development of the grounds harmonizing more with the surrounding environment.

OUR GROUNDS, OUR LOCALITY

Ask the children in Key Stage 2 to make a trail for children in Key Stage 1 to show the main differences and similarities between the school grounds and the local area. The trail should focus on features in the school grounds first, then go out into the local area to show similar features and those features that are different. The older pupils will need to consider such things as:

• safety;
• distance;
• how to show the features.

As a rehearsal, the children could use 'Viewpoints' software. This allows them to wander through an environment, choosing their route and taking photographs of their discoveries.

Children at Key Stage 2 could construct a diorama (a three-dimensional model) of the landscape seen from the school, looking outwards in a particular direction. It should include some of the surrounding locality and should emphasize both the similarities and the differences in the landscape between the school grounds and its surroundings.

The diorama can be constructed rather like theatre scenery in a cardboard box, as shown in the drawing below. (See also 'Using models' on page 9.)

BRINGING THE LOCALITY INTO SCHOOL

The locality of the school, meaning the area immediately around the school or encompassing the bulk of the children's homes, is a vital resource for pupils' learning in

A diorama of a view from the school grounds

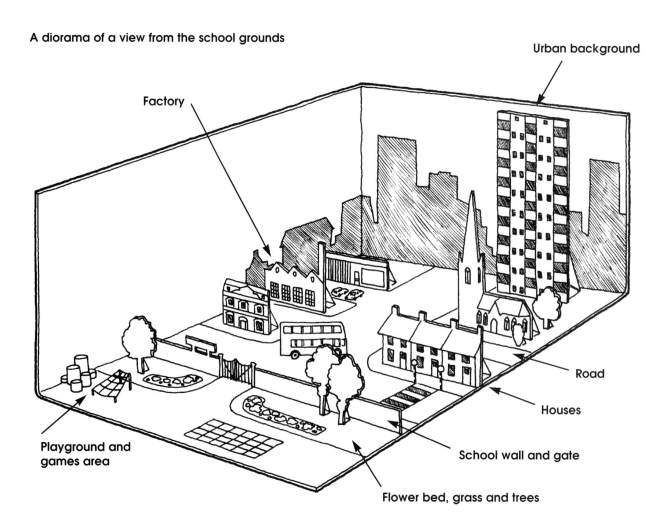

Geography. Although first-hand contact is necessary for effective learning, there are possibilities for 'bringing the local area into the school grounds'.

A PLAN OF A BUILDING

One way of doing this is to chalk or paint on the playground the floor plan of a well-known local building, like a sports hall or library, a church, mosque or synagogue, so that the children may learn through play or through class activities about spatial orientation, finding their way around features of the local environment. Ask them, for example, to:

- follow a route which you have made through the plan;
- make up routes for each other;
- chalk in features of the building;
- pretend they work there and to carry out their jobs in the building.

A LOCAL MAP

Similarly, chalking or painting on the ground a large-scale map of the local area, or at least the part surrounding the school, can reinforce visits to the school's locality. If it is intended to use models such as cars or houses

then the scale should be adjusted accordingly, though it only needs to be approximate. If children are to move around the map themselves, the chalked outline needs to be bigger.

On your chalked map of the area, mark in some local landmarks and ask the children to find others and perhaps the streets or homes of some individuals.

Give them tasks that involve finding things in the area shown on the map.

Ask the children to follow their journey to school, saying what they pass on the way. Older children can give each other instructions to move about the map or to extend the map or add more detail.

Children can take on the roles of people living or working in various places on the map and be challenged to explain their attitude to developments such as the building of a new leisure centre or a road-widening scheme. As an extension to this, the children can carry out developments themselves by wiping off the chalk in places and adding new features to the neighbourhood. They need to discuss the effects of such changes.

Some other ideas for geographical playground markings are explained in Chapter 2.

A cardboard model of a local shopping centre can be placed on the chalked map.

An outline map of Great Britain painted on the playground

SHOPPING

An additional feature is to model the local shopping centre from cardboard boxes. A touch of reality can be gained by taking photographs or using children's drawings of the actual shop fronts and pasting them on the boxes. Place the models on the chalked outline of the road system in their appropriate places. Children at Key Stage 1 can carry out shopping trips, deciding where certain goods can be bought.

At Key Stage 2, the pupils can work out the most efficient way of buying a shopping list of goods and measure the distances involved in different routes. If compass points are chalked on the ground near the outline map, the pupils can also follow or make instructions for routes using compass directions.

Using the grounds to help learn about distant places

Though the school grounds are very much a local environment, they can be used to contribute to children's learning about distant places. Knowledge of the location of places, for example, can be enhanced by maps of the United Kingdom, different continents or even the world painted on to the playground. Activities or playground games can be based on the outlines. The grounds can also be used to simulate features and conditions elsewhere in the world. Plants from different environments and cultures around the world can be planted; in fact, the origin of many of our garden plants makes an instructive, and often surprising, area for research. There is also scope for mapping out or even constructing houses or settlements from distant places. (For more ideas about developing the grounds for exotic plants see *People, Plants and Places* by Julian Agyeman.)

AN AWAYDAY IN THE U.K.

On the playground a large chalked or painted outline of your home region or the United Kingdom can be used at both key stages to reinforce knowledge of where places are located.

Give each child a ticket with the name of a major place within the region or the U.K., depending on your map, and ask them to go and stand on the correct spot. Get them to make rail journeys in order to swap with another place.

An alternative is to ask football teams from each town or city to 'play' each other, the 'away' team visiting the 'home' team.

THE WORLD'S OUR OYSTER

Using a chalked outline of a continent or the world, send children from one world city to another. They must 'fly' in a straight line across the map, naming the places they cross, including rivers, mountains and oceans, before landing at their destination.

Describe different climate types and ask the children to go to the place where they think they might experience each one.

Give instructions from base for children to 'sail' around the world's oceans in order to unload cargo at particular ports. Let the children take it in turns to give instructions to each other.

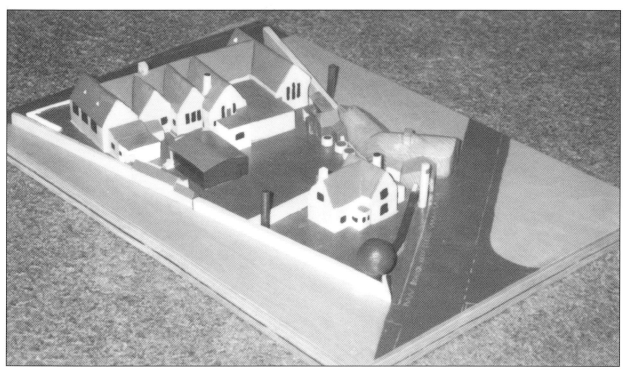

Starting with a model of the school, add surrounding features to help children develop a sense of locality.

FROM FAR TO NEAR

If you are studying a locality in a distant part of the world, such as an Indian village, chalk a large-scale outline map of that place on the playground to enable the children to simulate the lives of people who live there.

Move around the village or settlement to imitate the daily movements of people. Act out incidents or activities in the village, with children taking the parts. Give the children the opportunity to experience some of the differences from their own culture.

To introduce some reality, try carrying water from a standpipe to home or gather wood from far away in the grounds and bring it back to the village.

Introduce the field system by marking out the shapes on the field, if you have one. On a large enough site, you could mark out the true size of some of the buildings in the village and the extent of one family's holdings in the field. Simulating the lives of these people with other children watching could help to bring the distant place to life!

Try using a CD ROM that explores a distant place, such as 'Discover India', alongside the pretend settlement in the grounds.

Links between the activities and the Programmes of Study for Geography in the National Curriculum in England and Wales and the National Guidelines in Scotland

Chapter and Page No.	Activity	Geography PoS (England)	Environmental Studies P1 – 6 (Scotland)	Geography PoS (Wales)
Ch. 2 p.7	Signpost mapping	KS1: 1a, 3a, 3b, 3c, 3d, 5a KS2: 2b, 2c, 5a	Making and using maps	KS1: 1b, 2a, 2b, 2c KS2: 2b, 2c, 4a
p.8	A view from above	KS1: 3d	Making and using maps P1–3	KS1: 2d
p.9	Hunt the shape	KS1: 3b, 3d	Making and using maps	KS1:2b, 2c
p.9	Classroom model	KS1: 3c, 3d KS2: 1c, 3c, 3d	Making and using maps P1–3	KS1: 2c, 2d KS2: 2c
p.9	Playground model	KS1: 1a, 1b, 2, 3b, 3f, 5a KS2: 2a, 2b, 2c 3b, 3c, 3e	Making and using maps P1–3	KS1: 1a, 1b, 1c, 2b, 2c, 2d, 2e, 5a KS2: 1a, 1b, 1c, 2b, 2c, 2e
p.10	Blue monkey	KS1: 3d KS2: 3d	Making and using maps	KS1: 2d KS2: 2d
p.11	Helicopter flight	KS1: 1a, 1b, 2a, 2b, 2c, 2d, 2f, KS2: 1a, 1b, 2a, 2b, 2c, 3b, 3c, 3e	Making and using maps	KS1: 1a, 1b, 1c, 2b, 2e KS2: 1a, 1b, 1c, 2b, 2c, 2e
p.12	Photo spot	KS1: 1a, 1b, 3b, 3c, 3d, 3f KS2: 1a, 1b, 2a, 2b, 2c, 3b, 3c, 3e, 3f	Making and using maps/Aspects of physical and built environment/ IT	KS1: 1a, 1b, 1c, 2b, 2c, 2e, 2f, 5a KS2: 1a, 1b, 1c, 2b, 2c, 2d, 2e, 2f
pp.13,20	Picture mapping	KS1: 2, 3b, 3d, 3f	Making and using maps	KS1: 1a, 1b, 1c, 2b, 2c, 2e
p.13	Grids	KS1: 3c KS2: 3d	Making and using maps P4–6	KS1: 2d KS2: 2d
p.13	Colour bingo	KS1: 3c KS2: 3d	Making and using maps P4–6	KS1: 2d KS2: 2d
p.13	Playing with patterns	KS1: 3c KS2: 3d	Making and using maps P4–6	KS1: 2d KS2: 2d
p.14	Mapping a miniature school	KS1: 3c, 3e, 3f KS2: 3b, 3c, 3d, 3f	Making and using maps	KS1: 2c, 2d, 2f KS2: 2c, 2d, 2f
p.14	Signs and directions	KS1: 1a, 1b, 2, 3b 3c, 5a, 5b, 5c KS2: 1b, 2a, 2b, 2c, 3b, 3c, 3d, 3f	Locations, linkages and networks	KS1: 1a, 1b, 1c, 2b, 2c, 2f, 6e, 6f KS2: 1a, 1b, 1c 2b, 2c, 2d, 2f
p.15	Mazes	KS1: 3c	Making and using maps	KS1: 2d
p.15	Compass points	KS1: 3c KS2: 3d	Making and using maps	KS1: 2d KS2: 2d
p.16	Treasure hunt	KS1: 3b, 3c, 3e, 3f KS2: 3b, 3d	Making and using maps	KS1: 2b, 2d, 2e KS2: 2b, 2d, 2e
p.17	An orienteering course	KS2: 3c, 3d	Making and using maps	KS2: 2c, 2d
p.18	My world – my school	KS1: 3d, 3e, 3f KS2: 3c, 3d, 3f	Making and using maps/IT	KS1: 2c, 2d, 2f KS2: 2c, 2d, 2f
p.18	Routeways	KS1: 3d, 3e, 3f KS2: 3c, 3d, 3f	Locations, linkages and networks/ IT	KS1: 2c, 2d, 2f KS2: 2c, 2d, 2f

Chapter and Page No.	Activity	Geography PoS (England)	Environmental Studies P1–6 (Scotland)	Geography PoS (Wales)
p.18	Creating a toposcope	KS1: 1a, 3a, 3b, 3c, 3d, 3f, 5a KS2: 3b, 3c, 3d, 3e	Aspects of physical and built environment/the design process	KS1: 2a, 2b, 2c, 2e KS2: 2b, 2c, 2d, 2e
pp.15,21	Compass challenge	KS1: 3c, 3f KS2: 3d, 3e	Making and using maps	KS1: 2d, 2e KS2: 2d, 2e
Ch. 3 p.22	How does the weather affect people's behaviour?	KS1: 2, 5c KS2: 1b, 2, 8a	Ways places have affected people P1–3	KS1: 5b, 6b KS2: 1, 2b
p.23	Recording the weather	KS1: 2, 3a KS2: 2, 3b, 3f, 4, 8a	Aspects of physical and built environment/On planet Earth/IT	KS1: 1, 2b, 5a, 6a KS2: 1, 2b, 2f, 7a
p.24	Weather extremes in the school grounds	KS1: 2 KS2: 2, 3b, 3c, 3d, 8a	Ways places have affected people/On planet Earth	KS1: 1, 5b, 6b KS2: 1, 2b, 7a
p.25	A weather-friendly school?	KS1: 2, 3b, 5c KS2: 2, 3b, 3c, 8a	Ways places have affected people	KS1: 1, 2b, 5/6b KS2: 1, 2b, 2c, 7a
p.25	Seasons	KS1: 5c KS2: 1c, 8b	Ways places have affected people/On planet Earth P1–3	KS1: 6b KS2: 7b
p.26	Where does the water go?	KS2: 1b, 2, 3c, 3d, 3e, 7a	Ways places have affected people/On planet Earth	KS2: 1, 2b, 2c, 6a
p.27	How quickly does the water soak away?	KS2: 2, 3b, 3c, 3d	Ways places have affected people/On planet Earth	KS2: 1, 2b
p.28	Puddle trouble	KS1: 1b, 2	Ways places have affected people/On planet Earth	KS1: 1, 2b
p.28	Word mapping	KS1: 3a KS2: 3a	Aspects of physical and built environment	KS1: 2a KS2: 2a
p.29	Contouring	KS2: 1c, 3b, 3c, 3d	Aspects of physical and built environment	KS2: 2b, 2c
p.29	Looking out at other landforms	KS2: 2, 3a, 4, 5a	Aspects of physical and built environment	KS2: 1, 2d, 2e, 4a
Ch. 4 p.31	Who works in our school?	KS1: 1b, 2, 5d	Social groupings, social needs P1–3	KS1: 1, 2e, 5/6c
p.31	Profiling our community	KS2: 1a, 1b, 1c, 1d, 2, 3b, 3c, 3e, 3f, 4, 5a, 9b, 9c, 10a	Social groupings, social needs/IT	KS2: 1, 2e, 2f, 3, 4a 8a, 8b
p.34	Moving around the school	KS1: 1a, 2, 3b, 6a, 6b, 6c, KS2: 1, 2, 3, 4, 5a, 5c, 9c, 10a	Locations, linkages and networks/Making and using maps/IT	KS1: 1, 2b, 2c, 5d, 6d KS2: 1, 2, 3, 4a, 4b, 8c, 9a, 9b
p.35	The things people do	KS1: 2, 5d KS2: 1, 2, 3, 4, 5c, 10a	Ways people use places	KS1: 1, 2c, 5e, 6e, 5f, 6f KS2: 1, 2, 4a, 8, 9
p.35	Where do we play?	KS1: 1a, 2, 3b, 6a, 6b, 6c KS2: 1, 2, 3	Ways people use places/Social rules/Conflict and decision-making	KS1: 1, 2b, 2c, 5e, 6e, 5f, 6f KS2: 1, 2, 9b
p.36	Keeping the school tidy	KS1: 1b, 2, 3b, 6c KS2: 1, 2, 3, 10a, 10b	Ways people use places/Social rules	KS1: 1, 2b, 2c, 5f, 6f KS2: 1, 2, 9b
p.37	Skylines seen from the school grounds	KS1: 1a, 1c, 3b, 3f, 4, 5a KS2: 1, 3a, 3e, 3f, 4, 5, 9b	Aspects of physical and built environment	KS1: 2b, 2e, 4a, 4b, 4c, 4d, 5e, 6e KS2: 2, 4a, 8b

Chapter and Page No.	Activity	Geography PoS (England)	Environmental Studies P1–6 (Scotland)	Geography PoS (Wales)
p.37	Finding out about the local environment	KS1: 1a, 1b, 2, 3b, 3f, 4, 5a, 5d KS2: 1, 3a, 3c, 3d, 3e, 4, 5, 9	Aspects of physical and built environment	KS1: 2b, 2e, 4a, 4b, 4c, 4d, 5e, 6e KS2: 1, 2, 4b, 8b
p.39	Why here?	KS1: 1a, 1b, 2, 3d, 3e KS2: 1, 2, 3, 9a, 9b	Ways people use places/ Change and continuity	KS1: 1, 2d, 4c KS2: 1, 2, 4a, 8b, 9a
p.39	How has the site changed?	KS1: 1a, 1b, 2, 3f, 6b KS2: 1, 2, 3b, 3e, 5d 9	Ways people use places/Change and continuity	KS1: 1, 2e, 5f, 6f KS2: 1, 2, 4c
p.40	A history trail	KS1: 2, 6b	Historical evidence	KS1: 1, 5/6f
p.41	Car parking	KS1: 1a, 2, 3b, 6b, 6c KS2: 1, 2, 3b, 3e	Ways people use places	KS1: 1, 2b, 2e, 5e, 6e 5f, 6f KS2: 1, 2, 4b, 4c, 8c
p.41	Plotting land use on a map of the school site	KS2: 1, 2, 3a, 3b, 3c 3c, 3d, 3e, 3f, 9c	Making and using maps P4–6/ Ways people use places/IT	KS2: 1, 2, 8b, 8c, 9a, 9b
p.42	Wear and tear	KS2: 1, 2, 3, 10a	Ways people use places	KS2: 1, 2, 9a, 9b
Ch. 5 p.43	Are you smiling?	KS1: 6a	Ways places affect people	KS1: 1a, 1b, 2b, 4b, 6e
p.43	A rainbow map of feelings	KS2: 2a, 2b	Ways places affect people/Making and using maps P4–6	KS2: 1a, 1b, 2b, 2c
p.44	Why do we feel this way?	KS1: 1a, 1b, 2, 6a KS2: 1a, 1b, 2a, 2b, 2c	Ways places affect people	KS1: 1a, 1b, 1c, 2b 4b, 6e KS2: 1a, 1b, 1c, 2b, 9a
p.44	Nice or nasty?	KS1: 1a, 1b, 2, 3a, 3b, 5a, 6a KS2: 1b, 1c, 2a, 2b, 2c, 3b, 10a	Ways places affect people	KS1: 1a, 1b, 1c, 2b 6e KS2: 1a, 1b, 1c, 2b
p.45	A guide to the school grounds	KS2: 2a, 2b, 2c, 3a, 3c, 3f, 5a, 5d, 10b	Aspects of physical and built environment/IT	KS2: 1a, 1b, 1c, 2a, 2b, 2c, 9a, 9b
p.46	The school grounds calendar	KS1: 1a, 2, 3b, 3c, 5a, 6a KS2: 2a, 2b, 2c, 3a, 3b, 3f, 5a	Aspects of physical and built environment	KS1: 1a, 1b, 1c, 2a, 2b, 2c, 2e, 6e KS2: 1a, 1b, 1c, 2a, 2b
p.47	Is your site visitor friendly?	KS1: 1a, 1b, 2, 3a, 6a KS2: 1b, 1c, 2a, 2b, 2c, 3a, 3b, 5a, 10a	Ways places affect people/ Social groupings/the design process	KS1: 1a, 1b, 1c, 6e KS2: 1a, 1b, 1c, 2b, 9b
p.47	A word in your eye	KS1: 1a, 2, 3a KS2: 2a, 3a	Ways places affect people	KS1: 1a, 1b, 1c, 2b, 6e KS2: 2a
p.48	Poems and pictures	KS1: 1a, 2, 3a KS2: 3a	Ways places affect people	KS1: 1a, 2a KS2: 2a
p.49	Plants and their places	KS2: 1a, 2a, 2b, 2c, 3a, 3b, 3d, 3c, 8c	Variety of living things/Interaction of living things with environment	KS2: 1a, 1b, 1c, 2a, 2b, 2d, 2e, 7c
p.49	Improving the grounds for wildlife	KS2: 2a, 2b, 2c, 3a, 3b	Interaction of living things with environment	KS2: 1a, 1b, 1c, 2a, 2b
p.50	An African house	KS2: 2a, 2b, 2c, 3a, 3d	The design process/Social groupings	KS2: 1a, 1b, 1c, 2a, 2b
p.51	Planning geographical projects in the school grounds	KS2: 1b, 2a, 2b, 2c, 3b, 10a, 10b	The design process/Aspects of physical and built environment	KS2: 1a, 1b, 1c, 2b, 9a, 9b

Chapter and Page No.	Activity	Geography PoS (England)	Environmental Studies P1–6 (Scotland)	Geography PoS (Wales)
Ch. 6 p.56	Through the keyhole	KS1: 1a, 1b, 2, 3a, 3b, 3e, 5a, 5b	Ways places affect people	KS1: 1a, 1b, 1c, 2a, 2b, 4a, 4c
p.56	And on your right …	KS2: 1a, 1b, 2a, 2b, 2c, 3a, 5a	Aspects of physical and built environment P4–6	KS2: 1a, 1b, 1c, 2a, 4a
p.57	Celebrating a special place	KS1: 1a, 3d, 5a, 6c KS2: 10a, 10b	Ways places affect people/the design process	KS1: 1a, 1b, 1c, 2c, 2f, 6f KS2: 1a, 1b, 1c, 2c, 2e, 9b
p.58	Virtual reality walk	KS1: 3a, 3c, 3e, 5a KS2: 3a, 3d, 5a	Making and using maps	KS1: 2a, 2c, 4a KS2: 2a, 2c, 4a
p.58	Our elastic school	KS1: 1a, 1b, 2, 3a, 3d KS2: 1a, 1b, 1c, 2a, 3a, 3c, 5a	Making and using maps	KS1: 2a, 4a KS2: 2c, 4a
p.59	My special place	KS1: 1a, 1b, 2, 3a, 3b, 3d KS2: 1a, 1b, 2a, 2b, 3a, 3c, 5a	Ways places affect people/ Making and using maps	KS1: 1a, 1b, 1c, 2b, 2c KS2: 1a, 1b, 1c, 2b, 2c
p.59	Beating the bounds	KS1: 1a, 1b, 2, 3a, 3b, 3d, 5a KS2: 1a, 1b, 1c, 2a, 2b, 2c, 3a, 3b, 3c, 3d, 5a, 5c, 5d, 9b, 9c, 10a, 10b	Locations, linkages and networks	KS1: 1a, 1b, 1c, 2b KS2: 1a, 1b, 1c, 2a, 2b, 2c, 2e, 8b, 9a, 9b
p.61	Boundaries – the hidden messages	KS2: 1a, 1b, 2a, 2b, 2c, 3a, 5a, 10b	Locations, linkages and networks P4–6	KS2: 1a, 1b, 1c, 2b
p.61	Future shifts	KS2: 1a, 1b, 2a, 2b, 2c, 3a, 3b, 3c, 3d, 9b, 10b	Locations, linkages and networks/ Change and continuity P4–6	KS2: 1a, 1b, 1c, 2a, 2b, 2c, 8b
p.61	A place by post	KS1: 1a, 1b, 3a, 5a KS2: 3a, 5a, 5b	Ways places affect people	KS1: 1b, 1c, 2a KS2: 1b, 1c, 2a
p.62	Our grounds, our locality	KS2: 1a, 1c, 1d, 2a, 2b, 2c, 3a, 3c, 3f, 5a, 9b	Aspects of physical and built environment/IT	KS2: 1a, 1b, 1c, 2a, 2b, 2c, 2f, 8b
p.63	A plan of a building	KS1: 1a, 3a, 3c, 3d, 3e, 5a, 5d KS2: 1a, 3a, 3c, 3d, 5a, 5d	Making and using maps	KS1: 1a, 1b, 2a, 2c, 2d, 4a KS2: 1a, 1b, 2a, 2c, 2d 4a
p.63	A local map	KS1: 1a, 1b, 3a, 3b, 3c, 3d, 5a, 5d KS2: 1a, 1b, 3a, 3b, 3c, 3d, 5a, 5d	Making and using maps	KS1: 1a, 1b, 1c, 2a, 2b, 2c, 2d, 4a, 4c KS2: 1a, 1b, 1c, 2a, 2b, 2c, 2d, 4a, 4c
p.64	Shopping	KS1: 1a, 3a, 3b, 3c, 3d, 3e, 5a, 5d KS2: 1a, 3a, 3b, 3c, 3d, 3e, 5a, 5d, 9b	Economic organisation/Ways people use places	KS1: 2a, 2c, 2d, 2e, 4a, 4c KS2: 2a, 2c, 2d, 2e, 4a, 4b
p.64	An awayday in the U.K.	KS1: 3d KS2: 3d	Locations, linkages and networks	KS1: 2d KS2: 2d
p.64	The world's our oyster	KS1: 3d KS2: 3d	– –	KS1: 2d KS2: 2d
p.65	From far to near	KS1: 3a, 3c, 3d, 3f, 5b, 5d KS2: 3a, 3c, 3d, 3e, 3f 5b, 9a, 9b	Locations, linkages and networks	KS1: 2a, 2c, 2d, 2e, 4a, 4c, 4d, 6c KS2: 2a, 2c, 2d, 2e, 4d, 8e, 8f

Resources

USEFUL ORGANIZATIONS

Association for Science Education
College Lane
Hatfield AL10 9AA

Botanic Gardens Education Network
Descanso House
199 Kew Road
Richmond,
Surrey TW9 3BW

British Trust for Conservation Volunteers
36 St Mary's Street
Wallingford
Oxon OX10 0EJ

Centre for Alternative Technology
Llwyngwern Quarry
Machynlleth
Powys SY20 9AZ

Centre for World Development Education
1 Catton Street
London WC1R 4AB

Common Ground
c/o London Ecology Centre
45 Sheldon Street
London WC2 9HJ

Council for Environmental Education
School of Education
University of Reading
Reading
Berkshire RG1 5AQ

Development Education Association
3rd Floor,
29–31 Cowper Street
London EC2 4AP

Friends of the Earth
26-28 Underwood Street
London N1 7JQ

Geographical Association
343 Fulwood Road
Sheffield S10 3BP

Henry Doubleday Research Association
National Centre for Organic Gardening
Ryton on Dunsmore
Coventry CV8 3LG

Learning through Landscapes
Third Floor, Southside Offices
The Law Courts
Winchester
Hampshire SO23 9DL

National Association for Environmental
  Education
Wolverhampton Polytechnic
Walsall Campus
Gorway
Walsall
West Midlands WS1 3BD

National Association for Urban Studies
Lewis Cohen Urban Studies Centre
University of Brighton
68 Grand Parade
Brighton BN2 2JY

National Children's Play and Recreation Unit
359-361 Euston Road
London NW1 3AL

Ordnance Survey Education Team
Romsey Road
Southampton SO16 4GU
Tel: 01703 792795

Plantlife
Natural History Museum
Cromwell Road
London SW7 5DB

Religious Education and Environment
Project
8th Floor, Rodwell House
Middlesex Street
London E1 7HJ

Royal Society for the Protection of Birds
The Lodge
Sandy
Bedfordshire SG12 2DL

Science and Plants for Schools (SAPS)
Homerton College
Hills Road
Cambridge CB2 2PH

Soil Association
86 Colston Street
Bristol,
Avon BS1 4DZ

Survival International
310 Edgeware Road,
London W2 1DY

Tidy Britain Group
The Pier
Wigan WN3 4EX

Tree Council
51 Catherine Place
London SW1E 6DX

WATCH/Royal Society for Nature
Conservation
The Green
Witham Park
Waterside South
Lincoln LN5 7JR

World Wide Fund for Nature
Panda House
Weyside Park
Catteshall Lane
Godalming
Surrey GU7 1XR

A variety of useful charts are available from
Pictorial Charts Education Trust
27 Kirchen Road
London W13 0UD.

BOOKS AND OTHER PUBLICATIONS

J. Agyeman, *People, Plants and Places* (LTL/Southgate, 1995)

E. Ayensu, *Our Green and Living World* (CUP, 1984)

C. Baines, *How to Make a Wildlife Garden* (Elm Tree Books, 1985)

Birmingham Development Education Centre/ Birmingham Botanic Gardens Base, *Around the Garden in 80 Ways: Using Plants to Raise Develop- ment Issues at Key Stage 2* (1994)

Books for Keeps, *Green Guide to Children's Books* (1991)

C. Brickell (ed.), *The Gardeners' Encyclopedia of Plants and Flowers* (Dorling Kindersley, 1989)

M. Brown, *Growing Naturally* (Southgate/HDRA, 1996)

R. Clark and P. Walters, *Trees in the School Grounds* (Southgate/LTL, 1992)

J. Cochrane, *Plant Ecology* (Wayland, 1987)

M. Collins, *Urban Ecology: A Teacher's Resource Book* (Cambridge Educational, 1984)

Department for Education and Science, *The Outdoor Classroom (Building Bulletin 71) Educational Use, Landscape Design and Management of School Grounds* (HMSO/LTL/Southgate)

I. Edwards and K. McDonald, *Green Inheritance* (WWF UK, 1991)

J. Feltwell, *Recycling: A Practical Guide for the School Environment* (LTL/Southgate, 1991)

M. Grace, W. Lucas and J. Wood, *Esso Schoolwatch Pack* (LTL, 1993)

S. Greig et al., *Earthrights – Education as if the Planet Really Mattered* (WWF/Kogan Page, 1987)

International Bee Research Association, *Garden Plants Valuable to Bees* (1981)

J. Johnston and J. Newton, *Building Green – A Guide to Using Plants on Roofs, Walls and Pavements* (London Ecology Unit, 1993)

B. Keaney and W. Lucas, *The Outdoor Classroom (Bright Ideas)* (Scholastic/LTL, 1992)

Learning through Landscapes, *School Grounds Resource Directory* (LTL, 1994)

W. Lucas and A. Mountfield, *Fundraising for School Grounds* (LTL, 1995)

R. Mears, *The Survival Handbook* (Oxford Illustrated Press, 1990)

OFSTED Report, *Geography: A Review of Inspection Findings 1993/94* (HMSO, 1995)

M. Prime, *Plants for a Multicultural Garden* (London Borough of Lewisham, 1993)

RSPB/LTL, *Wildlife and the School Environment* (LTL, 1992)

W. Titman, *Special Places; Special People* (LTL/WWF, 1994)

M. Walters, *Wild and Garden Plants* (Harper-Collins, 1994)

J. Willison, *Educational Resources Catalogue for Botanic Gardens* (BGCS, 1990)

COMPUTER SOFTWARE

'Magpie' _ A multimedia authoring application program, use to build up your own information package. Available from: Longman Logotron, 124 Cambridge Science Park, Milton Road, Cambridge CB4 4ZS.

'My World' series, available for Acorn and PC, includes: 'My World 2 – Geography KS1'; 'My World 2 – Junior Map Reader'; 'My World 2 – Let's Explore Area'; 'My World 2 – Map Reading Senior' KS2/3; 'My World 2 – Technology and Design Around School'. Available from: SEMERC, 1 Broadbent Road, Watersheddings, Oldham OL1 4LB.
Also accessible through:
SEMERC centres in most LEAs.

'Number 62 Honeypot Lane', Derek Allen, 1992. Available from: The Resource Centre, 51 High Street, Kegworth, Derby DE74 2DA.

'Picture Point' database – very simple, KS1 friendly. 'Junior Pinpoint' database – KS2, design your own data sheets or questionnaires, computer analyses data and shows it in clear pictorial representation. Both available from Longman Logotron, as above.

'Viewpoints', Simon and Sue Hosler. Available from: Sherston Software, Swan Barton, Sherston, Malmesbury, Wilts. SN16 0LH.

'Weatherman' – Acorn Risc OS. Available from: HS Software, 56 Hendrefoilan Avenue, Sketty, Swansea SA2 7NB.

'Weather Station' – Acorn Risc OS. Available from AVP, School Hill Centre, Chepstow, Gwent NP6 5PH.

'Weather Watch' – Acorn Risc OS, Magnolia Soft. Available from AVP, as above.

'Weather Watch' database – for manual recording of weather measurements, suitable for KS2. Available from: Soft Teach Educational, Sturgess Farmhouse, Longbridge Deverill, Warminster BA12 7EA.

Concept Keyboard – A4 size, A3 size. Available from: SEMERC, as above.

'Discover India' CD-ROM, ActionAid, 1995 (Mac/PC 486/33MHz). Available from: ActionAid, Chataway House, Leach Road, Chard, Somerset TA20 1FA.

OTHER RESOURCES

Automatic weather stations
'Weather Reporter' – automatic data logging weather station, continuously records wind speed and direction, temperature, hours of sunshine and daylight, rainfall, pressure and humidity (for BBC, Archimedes, Nimbus, IBM). Available from: The Advisory Unit: Computers in Education, 126 Great North Road, Hatfield, Herts AL9 5JZ.

'The MJP Automatic Weather Station'. Available from: MJP Geopacks, PO Box 23, St Just, Cornwall TR19 7JS. Various kits and weather boards also available.

Programmable control toys
'Pixie' – small, table-top size, with built-in rechargeable battery. Suitable for early KS1. Available from: Swallow Systems, 134 Cock Lane, High Wycombe, Bucks. HP13 7EA.

'PIP' – larger, with more features than 'Pixie', includes sound keys, rechargeable battery. Available from: Swallow Systems, as above.

'Roamer' – larger, dome-shaped toy, more complicated programming possible, including sound. Available from: Valiant Technology Ltd, Valiant House, 3 Grange Mills, Weir Road, London SW12 0NE.

Sensory equipment
Equipment for measuring, and recording on to computer software, light, sound, temperature and pressure. Some types can be taken some distance from the computer and then brought back to transfer data to software. Produced by a number of companies, including:
Commotion Ltd, Unit 11, Tannery Road, Tonbridge, Kent TN9 1RF.
Data Harvest Educational Electronics, Woburn Lodge, Waterloo Road, Linslade, Leighton Buzzard, Beds. LU7 7NR.
Philip Harris Education, Lynn Lane, Shenstone, Lichfield, Staffs. WS14 0EE.

Video still camera
Canon 'ION' camera, now replaced by Canon RC260. Available from photographic shops. Some local authority suppliers and some software suppliers also sell these, possibly cheaper. If the video still camera is to be used in conjunction with a computer, i.e. to transfer pictures on to the screen, a digitiser is also needed. Available from all major stockists.